13

WOMEN

YOU

SHOULD

Never MARRY

and how every man can recognize them

MARY COLBERT

WORTHY

Library of Congress Control Number: 2015930268

Printed in the United States of America

15 16 17 18 19 vpi 8 7 6 5 4 3 2 1

I dedicate this book to my grandsons,
Caleb, Jaret, Olan, Braden, Dylan, and Timothy—
and to my one granddaughter,
who is the most precious little girl in the whole world.

I also want to thank my sons, DJ and Kyle,
who made amazing decisions with the choices
of their wives, Becky and Meredith.

And last but not least, to my wonderful husband, Don.
He is the most amazing man I ever met,
and I am so thankful to be his wife and his partner in life.

CONTENTS

ACKNOWLEDGMENTS

I could acknowledge all the women I have met through the years who inspired this book—women who tear down their families with their way of handling life—but I won't. Instead, I will give praise to the ones who inspired me to be a better person, wife, and mother.

My mother-in-law, Kitty, is a marvelous role model for any woman. I am so thankful for her support and love for the family and me.

My mother, Evelyn, who is in heaven now, raised eight children pretty much on her own since her husband was a career military man who was gone most of my childhood. I am thankful that my mom showed me how to be strong and to do whatever was necessary to keep a family intact.

Thank you to my three sisters, who have all turned out to be amazing women who love their families. They, like our mother, do whatever is necessary to keep their families together. My sister Debbie—who had a broken back in the tenth grade and overcame unbelievable pain and suffering—managed to graduate college despite undergoing two life-threatening back surgeries. For years she was an admired schoolteacher and continues to stay active and very involved in her family and her community.

My sister Pam, who is an RN, and my sister-in-law Kitze, who has a master's in speech pathology, both have brilliant minds. They inspire anyone to be the best they can be.

My sister Tamara, who could have been a famous country music singer with her outstanding voice that stops people in their tracks, instead focused her attention on raising her two children, who both graduated with top honors and served as class officers.

My sister-in-law Mary is married to my brother who is a pastor in Chappaqua, New York. Mary amazes me to this day at how diligent she is in her support of my brother and his ministry and yet still looks like she did the day they married more than forty years ago.

My sister-in-law Cindy has been the backbone and support of my brother David. She worked tirelessly putting my brother through college so he could earn his masters in business.

I could go on and on, filling many pages with the amazing and inspiring women God has surrounded me with. Thank you all for your part in helping me communicate the message of the Good Wife.

Thank you to all who helped me articulate this message in such a way that young men and old men alike will "get it." Thank you to the Worthy Books team for helping me put it all together. Thank you, Ted Squires, for believing I could do it. Thank you, Steve Strang, for allowing me to write the article that inspired this book.

Finally, I deeply appreciate my husband, Dr. Don Colbert, for all his hard work and his spirit of excellence, showing me a path to write. And thank you to my sons, Kyle and DJ, for being just who you are.

FOREWORD

by Dr. Don Colbert, MD

This book is a must-read for any man—young or old or in-between—who is considering marriage.

There is no doubt in my mind that I married the right woman for me. To everyone who knows her, Mary's insight, love for the Lord and for me, as well as her love for our family, is obvious. She has in many ways been the wind beneath my wings of success. She has been a faithful, loving, as well as hardworking partner. Anyone who really gets to know her adores her. Her personality and spiritual insight are captivating. She has the gifts of encouragement as well as correction. Mary has counseled and prayed with many of my patients. I trust her judgment and insight when it comes to people. Mary came from a large family; this afforded her a unique understanding of different kinds of personalities. This has well prepared her for ministry.

I have counseled hundreds of men, as well as women, who have married the wrong person. The consequences of these choices are heartbreaking. A great deal of these broken families could have been avoided. I have seen far too may men who never reach their full potential. Most of the time this happens because of marrying a much too needy or controlling woman.

Generally speaking, public attention is usually on what "bad men" are doing to destroy families. But the truth is that men need to be aware of the kinds of women they are dating and trained to make a wise choice when it comes to selecting a spouse. A man's focus should not just be on finding a wife, but on finding his partner in life.

This book is needed today, more than ever.

I also think this is a great book for women to read and take a closer look at themselves. As they read these chapters, women will be able to identify whether or not they are falling into some of these negative traits.

This book does an amazing job of outlining possible pitfalls that could derail any guy from achieving his full potential. I am confortable saying choosing who you plan to spend the rest of your life with is the second most important decision a person will ever make.

Although this book primarily points out the pitfalls of marrying the wrong woman, I realize it definitely goes both ways. Anyone can change, with the right instruction, love, and encouragement. However, any change begins with recognizing the need to change and then being willing to change.

I will make sure my grandsons read this book when it's time for the courting to begin. I suggest you do the same.

INTRODUCTION

Most folks who pick up this book will instinctively turn to the contents page. They'll be looking for something that relates to them. Single men will wonder, *Who are these vixens and how can I avoid them?* Single women will be curious and ask themselves, *Am I one of these?* Protective mothers will want to warn their sons, "Watch out for this one." And though I didn't write this for married men, a lot of the ones I know will recognize the women I've described and muse, "Wish I'd known then what I know now."

I've actually written this for single men who hope one day to be married. And, guys, I want to share one thing from my heart: I have struggled with some of the qualities of all thirteen of these women myself. (Well . . . maybe not "Married Mindy"!) I'm not pointing a finger at *other* dangerous, single-dimensional women. Rather, I've recognized these qualities within *myself* and the women I know, and I suspect that most women—who are being honest—have as well.

The women you'll read about in these pages—the ones who are simultaneously fictional and all too real—are women who've become defined by a negative quality. I don't believe that the woman who's entered a beauty pageant is necessarily superficial. Nor do I believe that the one who's outspoken is necessarily a critical bully. What I *have* recognized is that when people allow sin to take root, they can be shaped by that sin. That's the type of woman I'm describing in these pages—the one who's allowed this trait to become the defining characteristic of her personality.

I'm not writing this book to throw other women under the proverbial bus either. Rather, because I've seen the ways marriages have struggled under the weight of some of these character types, I'm wanting to caution the young men I know and love—and one day my sweet grandsons!—to make the best possible choice in a wife they can.

Honestly, I hope whatever your reason, you're reading this *before* you find yourself in a committed relationship. Something wacky happens to all of us when we're "in love." Perhaps to ensure the survival of the species, God created us with hormones that can cause us to overlook another's imperfections. And while that natural drive is indeed a good gift, it can at times cloud our judgment.

If you're not in a serious relationship right now, my prayer is that you'll hold these words in your heart until you need them. And I also pray that they will build into you the antennae you will need to discern the best possible choice for a mate.

If you *are* in a serious relationship with a woman you're considering marrying, hand this book to your roommate or brother or aunt. Immediately. Do not pass go; do not collect two hundred dollars. Gather the courage it takes to let people who love you chime in *honestly* about what they recognize in your beloved. Although conversations like this can be uncomfortable, I can't stress enough how important it is to be honest with yourself. If you give them permission, the people who love you will help you do this.

May the Lord bless you with wisdom as you seek to honor Him with all of your life.

—Mary

The heart of her husband safely trusts her;
So he will have no lack of gain.

—

Proverbs 31:11

1

BEWARE OF BLINDED BRENDA

When I arrived at the gym on Saturday morning, Brenda was climbing the StairMaster with fierce determination.

I won't lie: she looked fantastic.

Her light hair was pulled back in a lime scrunchie that coordinated with her halter top and workout pants. While sweat poured off nearby women and men, on Brenda it just sort of . . . glistened. Without a hint of makeup, she still looked like she'd stepped out of the pages of a women's fitness magazine. Seriously, her nails *and* the swoosh on her brand-new cross-trainers were lime green.

We'd taken some classes together over the years, so I paused to say hello.

"Hi, Brenda. How are you?"

"Well," she launched off, "the renovation on our lake house is delayed. Again!"

I tried to look like I cared.

She barreled on. "I told Bob he needs to drive up to the lake this week and light a fire under that crew."

"And he can take the time off work?" I queried.

"He says he can't, but I've already got a hair appointment on Monday, lunch with girlfriends on Tuesday, and a massage on Wednesday that I *really* need. I've got an appointment with this fabulous new masseur over on Main Street. I've heard he'll make me feel *great*. Then, unfortunately, my in-laws are coming for little Bobby's soccer tournament at the end of the week."

"Oh," I remarked, "is he enjoying soccer this year?"

"A better question would be, 'Am *I* enjoying it?' And the answer is no. He had a game this morning, but I skipped it because I just had to get this workout in. If I don't get in twelve hours of cardio each week, I am wrecked."

If I *got in* twelve hours of cardio, I'd be wrecked.

"That's where I'm headed," I offered, pointing across the room to the treadmills. "Have a good day."

I wanted some space from Brenda's pulsing diva energy. Somehow, no matter what we discussed, it was always all about Brenda.

UPSIDE-DOWN ORDER

Blinded Brenda is oblivious to the needs of others. Her world—although it technically involves a husband, children, friends, and others—centers on what she needs and wants.

You may have seen Brenda at a social function. She and her family usually arrive late. Her husband, who has patiently waited on her for forty-five minutes, looks harried. Her children, too, have been dragged along on the delayed train that always seems to run at Brenda's pace. But as she breezes into the room, every hair in place, Brenda seems unconcerned about either her family or her tardiness. Because, of course, while no one else's needs have been considered, Brenda's gotten everything she wanted.

In most areas of her life, Brenda expects instant gratification. If she sees a new designer dress in a catalog, she orders it within minutes. If she decides she wants a degree in celebrity photography or discovers a two-week Caribbean yoga cruise, she registers immediately, seemingly unaware of the impact her actions might have on anyone else. Even at church she feels entitled to step to the front of the line for a cup of coffee.

In some cases, Blinded Brenda was that young girl who was always treated as Daddy's little princess. She got whatever she wanted, whenever she wanted it.

Now, I have nothing against a girl who is Daddy's little

girl, but when she's in her twenties and still talking about being Daddy's little girl, something may be off. If this sounds like a woman you're close to, you might consider letting her know, in the most polite way, "Honey, I'm glad you're your daddy's little girl, but I'm looking for a woman. I'm looking for a woman who wants to be a *wife*, not a woman who wants to stay Daddy's little girl." Unfortunately, women who see themselves as Daddy's little girl often make very poor wives.

Brenda is chronically unable to see things from someone else's point of view. She can only see things from her viewpoint. For example, she is so absorbed in her enjoyment of a new lake home that she seems oblivious to the cost to her husband if he's absent from work. (I'd love to see this guy suggest that Brenda take care of cleaning the lake house!) Rather than recognizing the importance of being present with her children and the things that are meaningful to them, she sees only her own desire to hit the gym. Though Brenda's keenly aware of the ways she is affected by the world around her, she's less cognizant of how her actions impact others.

NOTE TO SINGLE MEN

Gentlemen, squint your eyes and peer into the future. Can you see the life you will share with the woman you're considering marrying? Can she? Neglecting to notice the trajectory of a woman's vision for the future—both hers and yours—is a mistake a lot of young men make. When the two of you gaze into the future together, do you both see the same thing? Do you see the woman God created her to be, and does she see the man God made you to be?

In the absence of your own personal magical crystal ball, one of the best ways to see into the future is to take your cues from the present. Right now, does the woman you're considering marrying notice the needs of others? Does she have to be the center of attention? Is she able to see what you might need or want? Right now you might be full of grace and patience for a girlfriend who seems to put herself first, but if this is a woman who will spend the next five or six decades *testing* that patience, you might want to slow down your relationship.

In Ephesians 5, Paul described a marriage in which a man and woman love one another the way Christ loved the church. Don't miss that! That's a radical love that sacrifices its own life for the other. Brenda, though, behaves as if her husband is her errand boy. Not only does she not bend her will to serve him, but she also behaves as if he exists only to serve her.

MEET THE ANTI-BRENDA

Are you familiar with the iconic "Proverbs 31 Woman"? She is nothing if not a powerhouse. I know a lot of women look to the qualities Solomon described in Proverbs 31 and feel dwarfed by this superhero of a woman. I've got good news for them, and I hope for men as well.

Solomon was not married monogamously as men are to-day. Because he had a host of concubines, the descriptors in this illustrious passage are therefore actually describing a combination of women. So if any women are sneak-reading this book, the pressure is off! (*Whew!*) And I hope the pressure will be off you guys as well, because trying to find this exact woman would be a lifelong search. She doesn't exist. You won't find her, because she is a fantasy.

Rather, Solomon gathered qualities from his different experiences of women to craft what is essentially a wish list. It gives a picture of the type of woman who makes a good wife. (If women made a similar wish list for the ideal husband, the superhero who would take shape would look a great deal like Jesus.) No woman will have all of the Proverbs 31 qualities in spades, but they're great markers to help you recognize the woman who's prepared and well equipped to be your wife. So we'll be taking a look at them as we work our way through this book.

The woman Solomon described is the kind of Good Wife who's very different from Brenda. To say that this Good Wife isn't all about herself doesn't necessarily make her a slave to others. Rather, this woman is savvy. She knows how to handle money. She knows how to supervise workers. She manages her home and—whether she pulls out her own feather duster or hires someone who has their own feather duster— she makes sure everything runs smoothly. She doesn't need to be up at 5 a.m. vacuuming, but she's not sleeping until noon either. She doesn't spend all her days at the mall or the spa. She's responsible and runs her home the way she'd run an efficient business.

Specifically, the woman Solomon describes is nothing like Brenda. While Brenda expects the world to revolve around her, the Good Wife is keenly attentive to the needs of others. That doesn't mean she's weak or subservient. Solomon painted her as a very capable, gifted woman who—like Christ—chooses to be *for* others.

ANOTHER TYPE OF WOMAN

In stark relief to Blinded Brenda and the other women detailed throughout this book, I'd like for you to catch a glimpse of the kind of woman you *do* want to marry. All of us—because we're human and sinful—have some of Blinded Brenda (and the rest) in us. I know there have been times when the Spirit has had to open my eyes for me to be aware of the needs of those around me. But while no woman is perfect, you can certainly set your sights on the type of wife God intended when He created the first woman from Adam's rib. God's intention for marriage was a good one, and as much as I want to warn you about some women to avoid, I also want you to begin to notice the kind of woman God has designed for you.

One godly woman, who is a healthy countertype to

Blinded Brenda, is Mary, the mother of Jesus. Mary's attitude, even as a young teenage girl, was quite remarkable. Rather than clinging to her own desires—because no girl in the ancient Near East would have chosen to be an unwed mother—she was able to release them in submission to the will of God with the confident affirmation, "Behold the maidservant of the Lord. Let it be to me according to your word" (Luke 1:38). Mary was willing to submit to God, in the most absurd and difficult circumstances, for a corporate good greater than her own. She was willing to endure humiliation and gossip, and she was prepared to release the hopes and dreams she'd had for a future that did not include the world's most outrageous surprise.

Mary sounds radically different from Brenda, doesn't she?

Blinded Brenda doesn't have the ability to see beyond her own needs and wants. While on one hand she's made herself very large in relation to others, the vision she has for her life is actually very small. She can't see herself being used, in any way, for the greater good. It is, and always will be, all about Brenda. Sadly, she lives with the Me-My-I Syndrome. You'll hear hints of it in conversation with her as she wails, "Well, that doesn't work for *me*. That really wouldn't be *my* choice. *I* want to do this, see that, and have the other."

Be careful of someone who can't see beyond her own wants and needs. This approach to living is like a deep hole that never gets filled.

Unlike Brenda, Mary was willing to submit to the Holy Spirit, trusting that her life's outcome would be exactly what God intended for it to be. Some today are quick to call any sort of submission "weakness," but Mary's submission was actually a demonstration of a remarkable strength. Mary knew that her life mattered and that it was important, but what was more important was how her life could be used for something greater than herself.

Does the woman you are considering marrying recognize something greater than herself, which is the work of Someone greater than herself?

A woman who is not "all about herself" does not mean she has no life at all. Or even that her life has been absorbed into her husband's life. Rather, it means that the Source of her life is actually found neither in herself nor in her husband but is rooted in her relationship with the Lord. I strive to make that true of myself as a wife to Don. Being led by God means that I've been set free from being all about me to become the wife I was created to be.

GLIMPSE THE ANTI-BRENDA

My daughter-in-law Becky is a great example of the anti-Brenda. Becky is a hairdresser and runs her own business. She keeps track of the household finances and is careful not to overspend. She takes notice of whether the house and clothes are clean. She keeps track of birthdays and anniversaries and reminds my son (even if it's her own birthday or their own anniversary!). She really is amazing.

If Becky were all about Becky, she'd insist on designer clothing. She'd demand flashy new jewelry. Her home would be custom decorated with the best of everything. She'd need a brand-new car each year. She might even insist on designer clothes for the kids so that they would reflect well on her. But Becky's priorities instead are to make sure that everyone in the household is cared for.

Here's an example: Becky recently planned a weekend getaway for her and my son, DJ. She arranged child care for the kids, and she made reservations and plans to do fun things together. In her thoughtful way, Becky was able to show DJ that he's important to her. She does it every day, in a million different ways.

Becky is the mother of three children: two boys and a little girl we call our "up" baby. Kate was born with Trisomy 21, known as Down syndrome. Her heart had only two chambers and one valve. Long story short, with prayer and nothing short of a miracle, today Kate is in first grade. She loves dance, and unless you know, looking at Kate you can hardly tell she has come through such an incredible miracle. That's why we call her our "up" baby. We refuse to call her "Down," because she is anything but down. Although Becky and DJ have been through some very hard times, she has managed to keep it all together and is still going strong.

Becky lives a life of service to others, yet she has a healthy confidence in herself. I hope you can see that the woman whose life is not centered on herself isn't a weakling or a pushover. She's a strong woman who's able to live *for* others, especially her husband.

A WOMAN NOT BLINDED TO THE NEEDS OF THOSE AROUND HER

When Cheryl Salem was eleven years old, she was in a terrible car accident that left her physically broken and scarred. While the challenges Cheryl faced might have driven another woman into the shadows, Cheryl went on to compete in pageants, winning the titles (among others) of Miss Mississippi in 1979 and Miss America in 1980. Cheryl really is a remarkable woman.

Cheryl and her husband, Harry Salem, had a precious daughter, Gabrielle, who was diagnosed with an inoperable brain tumor. Three days before their sweet Gabrielle died, Don and I visited the Salems' home. I was so struck during that visit by the way Cheryl never succumbed to self-pity. Rather, in the most difficult circumstances, her eyes were open to the needs of others.

Not only was my friend Cheryl attentive to her husband and her sons, but she was even buzzing about their home caring for her guests. I can still hear her asking, "Is there something you need?" The striking contrast between Cheryl's beauty—that never seemed to consume her—and the way she set her eyes on the needs of others made a lasting impression on me.

The woman to marry is the one, like Cheryl, like Becky, whose eyes are open to the needs of those around her.

STOP, PAUSE, OR GO?

Whether you're just beginning to imagine the kind of woman you'd like to marry, dating casually, or have an engagement ring burning a hole in your pocket, pay attention to the following signals.

RED FLAG

- Her conversation is sprinkled with lots of "I," "me," and "my."
- She is only able to see things from her own point of view.
- Her needs take priority over the needs of others.

YELLOW FLAG

- She identifies herself as "Daddy's little princess."
- She doesn't see the same future you envision.
- She doesn't mind inconveniencing others.

GREEN FLAG

- She has a clear vision of the man you were created to be.
- She longs to partner with you as a helpmate.
- She considers the needs of others.

Her children rise up and call her blessed;
Her husband also, and he praises her.

—

Proverbs 31:28

2

DITCH DOMINATING DONNA

Donna, a few other women, and I were meeting in Donna's living room to plan a community event. After we'd wrapped up our business and were chatting, Donna's husband, Dave, walked through the front door. On the way home from work he'd picked up their twins from soccer. The boys tromped up the stairs arguing with one another while he juggled his briefcase, cell phone, and a stack of files from the office. One glance at Dave's haggard face told me that he had had a rough day.

Before she greeted Dave or gave us a chance to, Donna sized him up and demanded, "Where's the milk?!"

The awkward glances on the couch where I sat let me know I wasn't the only one feeling uncomfortable at witnessing the strained marital moment.

I'm pretty sure I saw a little cartoon lightbulb turn on over Dave's head as he remembered that he'd forgotten to pick up milk on the way home. "Oh no!" he gasped. Fear flashed across his face before he dropped his work on the coffee table, turned on his heel, and left to get milk.

"That man!" Donna bellowed in our direction. "He would lose his head if it wasn't tied on!"

I was hoping her rant would end there, but it didn't.

"One thing. I ask him to do one thing. How hard is it to pick up a gallon of milk?"

None of us dared to answer. I knew I'd forgotten milk a few days earlier, and I suspected the same common faux pas might have silenced others as well.

Donna continued, "I cook a nice meal, and he's late for dinner. I make reservations at a restaurant, and he forgets. It's almost like he doesn't even *want* to be here."

I could believe it! The forgotten gallon of milk had escalated quickly into Dave being a pretty horrible monster. While Donna tried to compose herself, I just kept thinking, *Don't cry over spilt milk.* Or in this case, *Don't scream over forgotten milk.*

DON'T MESS WITH DONNA

On my drive home, I thought about Donna's fiery reaction. It was almost as if she was yelling at someone who wasn't even in the room. And because I know Donna, I think that might actually have been true.

Donna's father left home when she was a girl. He would come around occasionally during her childhood but wasn't reliable at all. When she married, she had hopes that Dave would fill the hole in her heart. And yet—as Dave quickly discovered in their marriage—nothing he did could heal the gaping wound her father had inflicted. Unhealed, she expected men to behave toward her as her father had. And even when they were really good guys, like Dave, she magnified their failings as if to squeeze them into a dad-shaped mold.

I want to be very clear: not every woman who has a father who failed her is a Dominating Donna. I know plenty of women who've had fathers who left them or were verbally and even physically abusive, and they aren't domineering women like Donna. Rather, these women have allowed God to heal the deep hurts of their hearts so that they can give and receive love freely. When they've allowed the Spirit to minister to their deepest needs, they've been freed to enter into healthy relationships with others.

Unfortunately, Donna isn't one of these women.

Instead, Donna treats her husband as if she can't even see the man who's standing in front of her and—with odd, cracked spectacles—sees only the man who left her and her mother. So daily she holds Dave's feet to the fire, demanding he prove he's not like her father. That he's not unreliable. She expects her husband to fail and gives him lots of opportunities to do it. And sadly, because Donna is dead set on gathering evidence to prove that her husband is like the man who hurt her, Dave doesn't stand a chance.

The look I saw on Dave's face, that flash of fear for the impending wrath he'd grown to expect, was one I've seen before. In their marriage, the proverbial spilt milk had become a tsunami of overreaction. Because she has trouble keeping things in perspective, Donna takes the smallest molehill and makes it into a mountain of woe for Dave. The little errors that spouses must learn to overlook—a forgotten errand, not texting when delayed—are instead recorded like a laundry list of failings. Then when he *does* fail, Donna punishes him (after the yelling) by giving him the silent treatment. (He, of course, receives this silence as a gift rather than punishment. Don't tell her.)

LISTEN WELL, MEN

If you're dating someone like Donna, notice the ways she uses her words. What is inside a woman can often be recognized by what comes out of her mouth. In fact, when Jesus was teaching His disciples that a tree can be known by its fruit, He counseled, "For out of the abundance of the heart the mouth speaks" (Matthew 12:34). That means that the inner character of a woman is evident in the way that she speaks. This is a great barometer not only for identifying Dominating Donna but her friends, like Blinded Brenda, as well.

Your girlfriend's words might not sound exactly like my friend Donna's harsh judgments. Perhaps instead you've heard her playfully joke, "You remind me of my dad." Chances are you already know whether that's something that bodes well for you or whether it's a sore spot in her heart. As they say, "Many a true word is spoken in jest." Listen for playful barbs that might indicate Donna isn't able to see you for *you*.

Also notice what happens when you do err. Maybe you forgot to take care of an errand while she was busy at work. Maybe you forgot your two-week date-iversary. Notice how she reacts to your faults and foibles. This isn't a test that she will pass or fail. I'm simply inviting you to notice how she reacts in real-life situations.

If this is a woman you're considering marrying, pay attention:

- Is she filled with grace?
- Does she try to understand your situation?
- Does she calmly ask for something different next time?
- Does she pout?
- Does she throw a fit?

- Does she give you the silent treatment?
- Does she try to manipulate with tears?

I also encourage you to notice how she reports your failings to her mother or to a girlfriend. Does she recognize that everyone makes mistakes? Or does she belittle you when she recounts what happened?

You might also consider asking others who know you both what they see and hear. Does a mutual friend experience Donna as someone who's gracious and thoughtful and levelheaded? Have your siblings—or hers—had difficulty interacting with her? Has she offended or ostracized your friends? While it may be tempting to overlook some of these signs when under the spell of romance, they actually serve as valuable indicators about the person you're considering marrying. The woman you're dating might not let loose like I saw Donna do with her husband. But if you pay attention to her character, to the way she uses words, to the way she responds to disappointment, you'll get a glimpse into the kind of wife she'll be to you.

THE WOMAN WHO'S CALLED BLESSED

When Solomon pieced together the ideal wife, he noted, "Her children rise up and call her blessed; / Her husband also, and he praises her" (Proverbs 31:28).

I'll bet you a gallon of milk it isn't easy for Donna's children to call her blessed or to praise her.

The type of woman who is called blessed by her husband and children is one who treats them with dignity and respect. This might sound like, "Hey, babe, if you know you're going to be late, just shoot me a text."

The woman who's valued and praised by her family is one who exercises understanding and reason with them: "No milk? No worries. The kids can have a breakfast bar in the morning, and I'll grab some milk on the way home from the office tomorrow."

As you think forward to the kind of woman you hope to marry, this is a great exercise: when you envision the future you'll share twenty or thirty years down the road, can you see yourself and your eventual children praising and blessing her?

A BIBLICAL MODEL

While Donna dominates with her words, the Good Wife meets conflict with thoughtfulness, maturity, and reason.

First Samuel 25 describes a woman with just this sort of wisdom. Abigail was the beautiful wife of an ornery and wicked man named Nabal. When David—whose servants had guarded and protected Nabal's shepherds—asked Nabal to extend hospitality to him and his men, Nabal insulted

David and blew him off. David, who'd been anointed king but had not yet taken office, would not stand for the insult. He and his men began to prepare for battle.

When Abigail caught wind of the conflict, she knew she had to act swiftly. Without her husband's knowledge, she loaded a great feast onto donkeys and sent servants with it to intercept David and his men on the road. With wise words she doused conflict, saying, "Hey, don't worry 'bout that ol' Nabal. What does he know? You are going to make a fabulous king, David. The Lord is going to exalt you and prosper you, just like He's promised. So why have needless bloodshed on your hands? That's all I'm sayin'" (1 Samuel 25:23–31, more or less).

Abigail—who was probably all too familiar with her husband's ill temper—might have thrown gasoline on his rude, fiery response to David. But in reacting thoughtfully and extending flattery and a feast to the soon-to-be king and his four hundred soldiers, Abigail saved the lives of many.

And *that* is how you make a molehill out of a mountain.

Every relationship will have its share of conflict and failings. The Good Wife acts with wisdom to minimize fallout rather than create more of it.

A WOMAN WHO BUILDS UP, NOT TEARS DOWN

When my friend Barb married her husband, Joe, twenty-five years ago, a lot of folks thought they were an odd match.

Joe was a fraternity guy and the life of every party. He was a real clown. Barb, though, was serious and studious. She was studying nursing and had known since she was a girl that she wanted to specialize in pediatric oncology.

Barb believes that despite their external differences, the Lord brought her and Joe together. It's been fun to watch how their relationship has grown and matured over the years since they drove away from their wedding reception in the souped-up orange 1978 Volkswagen Beetle his frat brothers had decorated for them.

One of the things I've noticed is that I've never heard Barb say an ill word about Joe. (And not because he suddenly became an angel either!) When Joe recently lost his job as a graphic designer and decided to work from home as a freelance web designer, Barb was as supportive as she could be. Not every woman would be similarly inclined. Though many would be more like Dominating Donna, Barb has poured her energy into supporting and building up her husband. And while each acknowledged the risks of the arrangement, Barb has had nothing but kind words to say about Joe's talent and her confidence that he'll make it a success. Right now they're both glad Barb's nursing job is paying the mortgage each month, but when Joe's business takes off, I think it will be—in large part—because he married a wife who has invested her heart and confidence in him.

AN ENCOURAGER

Dominating Donna is highly critical of her husband, but one godly woman I know who resisted this temptation is Pauline Harthern. Married for more than sixty years to pastor and evangelist Roy Harthern, Pauline gave her husband permission to be who he was. That's not to say that he never fell short or made bad decisions. Like all of us, he did. But when she might easily have become critical of her husband, like Dominating Donna, Pauline stayed by his side and encouraged him to become a better man. Pauline allowed Roy to be Roy, which is something Dominating Donna can't do. Donna is so tied up in how her husband's actions affect her and reflect on her that she's always trying to change him. Pauline, though, is so comfortable in her own skin that she was able to extend incredible grace to her husband.

STOP, PAUSE, OR GO?

As you consider the kind of wife you'd like to spend six or seven decades with, seek out a woman who will build you up and not tear you down. Choose one whose words are a source of fruitfulness and not decay.

RED FLAG 🏴

- She feels men have failed her, and that hurt still aches and throbs.
- She *expects* you to fail her.
- She responds with criticism and negativity when you err.

YELLOW FLAG 🏴

- She jokes that you're like the man who failed her.
- She makes small conflicts into gigantic ones.
- She responds to conflict with immaturity.

GREEN FLAG 🏴

- She extends grace and compassion when you make an honest mistake.
- She can calmly share her disappointment and move past it.
- She offers a reasonable solution for the next time you're in the same spot.

Charm is deceitful and beauty is passing,
But a woman who fears the LORD, she shall be praised.
—

Proverbs 31:30

3

HASTEN FROM HOLY HOLLY

I met Holly on a women's retreat in the mountains. We'd been placed together in a small group and were the first ones to gather in the meeting room our group had been assigned to. I dropped into a comfortable sofa, and Holly pulled a chair into the circle of furniture.

"Hi, I'm Mary," I offered.

"I'm Holly," she replied. "Nice to meet you."

"Hasn't this been a lovely weekend?" I ventured. The mornings and evenings had been cool and crisp, but the sun had burned off the chill during the daytime. "The weather has just been gorgeous. Certainly a lot different from Orlando, where I'm from!"

"Well," Holly explained, "I've been petitioning the Lord for beautiful weather all week. The Word promises that He hears the prayers of His people."

I chuckled at her Psalm 34 reference, but then noticed Holly wasn't smiling.

"Have you been here before?" she asked.

"No," I admitted, "I haven't."

"Well," Holly explained, "there are two ways up the mountain. Each year, before I come, I pray about which path to take. Yesterday I sat in my driveway for two hours waiting on the Lord before I was released to travel."

"Wow," I said in surprise. I couldn't imagine sitting in my driveway for two hours unless both my legs were broken.

Holly continued, "Mary, the Lord blessed that time."

I could believe that. My life is as full and busy as the next gal's, and I could imagine that being still with the Lord for an extended period would be, like Holly had experienced, a gift. I made a mental note to cushion my next road trip with a few extra driveway minutes on each end.

I wanted to hear more. Had God spoken to Holly's spirit? Had He taught her through His Word? Had He moved her to more fully love and bless her neighbors?

"Now I'm curious," I confessed. "How did the Lord meet you yesterday?"

Holly looked pleased that I'd asked. "For the first hour, God was silent," she began.

Ouch. I'd been there. Well, maybe not in the driveway, but in the silence.

"But I was not moving one inch until I was directed by the Lord," Holly explained.

Because I've experienced seasons when the Lord seemed quiet, I wasn't sure I could have made the same vow. Not if I wanted to make it to the mountaintop retreat, anyway.

"Finally," Holly announced, "the Lord spoke."

Now I was on the edge of my seat. What had God said to Holly? Had He charged her with leading a people to freedom the way He'd led Moses? Had He promised to bless many nations through her as He had Abraham? Had He at last answered her fervent prayers the way He had with Hannah?

"He told me to take Berger's Pass."

Two hours to connect to divine GPS?! Since she'd spent a week ordering up the great weekend weather, perhaps two hours for a map up the mountain felt like a bargain to Holly.

Other women had begun to gather in the meeting space. One, overhearing our conversation, chimed in, "We took State Road 38, the one that weaves through Rocky Hollow. Actually, we had two cars driving up from our church. The car that took Berger's Pass beat us by forty-five minutes because we were right behind a car that lost control and slid off the road."

It was evident from the proud glow on her face that word of this accident pleased Holly. It was less clear to me whether she'd done the math to realize that, with the driveway delay, she was still an hour and a quarter in the hole.

"Oh dear," I gasped. "I'm so sorry. Were they all right?"

"Well, I think they will be," the woman explained. "The driver swerved to avoid hitting a rabbit and skidded off the road. We pulled over to check on the passengers. It was a mom with three kids, all in car seats. The mama was pretty shaken up. So while Sandra, a nurse in our car, spoke to the mom and helped her call for assistance, the rest of us raided the snack cooler and craft basket we'd brought for the retreat to occupy the kids."

"Well," I confirmed, "I'm so glad you were there to help."

Holly was still beaming when she interjected, "They arrived after I'd already checked into my room and unloaded my bags. So if the Lord hadn't led me to take Berger's Pass, I would have crossed paths with the same rabbit!"

The leader of our small group arrived and called for our attention. As the group settled in, I had to wonder if it was just as likely the Lord led the group who drove through Rocky Hollow so they could help a family in need. I suspected it was.

Maybe more so.

WHAT'S SO HOLY ABOUT HOLLY?

It seemed more than a little sad to me that Holly counted avoiding a situation where God used His people to bless others as a win rather than a loss. But Holy Holly values the *appearance* of righteousness more than she does actually living a life of love. Holly doesn't just make a show of praying for driving directions. She'll let you know that she has sought the Lord's guidance about which supermarket to frequent on any given day, where to go out for dinner, and which movie to watch afterward. And if she gets a good parking spot at the movie theater, she'll let you know that it was God who gave it to her. (Because maybe God doesn't appreciate a good, brisk walk from the undesirable spaces?)

I don't begrudge Holly for tipping her face toward the Lord's countenance for guidance. Christians are called to make every thought—even, I suppose, ones that involve driving directions—captive to Christ. The rub comes with Holly's need to *appear* super spiritual. In fact, she never misses an opportunity to let you know that she's a wee bit *more* spiritually devoted than you are.

Sadly, there is no lightness or levity or wonder with Holly. She is dead serious. And while she may be very familiar with the Scriptures, she is bound by the law rather than freed by grace. Holly has little humor or joy in life.

Although Holly presents herself as a woman who trusts God, the polar opposite is frequently more true. Too often, Holly is bound by fear. Rather than moving forward to live a life of liberty, obeying Christ's call to love God and love people, Holly is afraid to experience a life of fullness and freedom. Rather than living in the confidence that she's held and loved and protected by God, Holly is often more aware of the devil's wily schemes. Strapped with fear, she'll spend more energy dodging evil and blaming the devil for life's mishaps than actually moving into the world with God.

While I was initially impressed with Holly's commitment to driveway discernment, over the course of our weekend together I began to realize that her fear of disappointing God—by taking the "wrong" route or choosing the "wrong" restaurant or walking an extra hundred yards to the theater—was actually unhealthy. Because she's controlled by the fear of disappointing God, Holly's appearance of super spirituality more often borders on *superstition*.

PRACTICE DISCERNMENT

Men, I want to be clear on this: you want to marry a woman who trusts God and listens for His voice. The Holly I've described, however, only presents the appearance of trust while actually being driven by fear.

I recognize the appeal. Who wouldn't want to be with someone who receives divine downloads? But I'd love to offer you a few tools to help with discernment. For starters, does a woman's relationship with God drive her into the world that He loves—full of broken people in need of love, hope, and redemption—or does it remove her from it? Is she living and tasting and building the kingdom Jesus ushered in, or does she spend more energy dodging the devil? Is her spiritual language matched by living out a vibrant life of faith? Does she ever quietly serve without announcing it and drawing attention to herself?

God doesn't want puppets. His plan is neither to control us by pulling strings from the heavens nor control us the way a ten-year-old boy controls a shiny red remote-control car. God has given us the freedom and creativity to choose whether to shop at Albertsons or Costco. As a result of our personal intimacy with the Lord, He sets us free to live and love boldly. He gives us work to do and is with us as we do it.

The tragic fallacy in Holly's thinking is that she believed she could make a mistake and take the wrong road to the mountains. This kind of theological thinking is driven by fear and not by faith. Men, the woman you want to marry is one with a deep, abiding faith in God. And that deep faith expresses itself in a willingness to trust that God is present with us on life's smooth, sunny highways and also that He is with us and for us in the stormy hollows when vans slide off the road, when moms are scared, and when kids are hungry.

Men, you want a woman who trusts God. Who will pray with you as you consider major life changes. Who will trust God's Spirit and leading in you just as you will trust the same in her.

THE FEAR THAT VANQUISHES FEAR

When Solomon described the Good Wife, he made a point to distinguish those qualities that are external and those that are internal: "Charm is deceitful and beauty is passing, / But a woman who fears the LORD, she shall be praised" (Proverbs 31:30). What's most beautiful, he was announcing, was the heart of a woman who feared and trusted God.

Wait, "fears the LORD"? Solomon! Holy Holly is afraid, and I thought I wanted to avoid that!

The Hebrew word יְרַ֖את (*yi-rat*) is the adjective Solomon used to describe the godly woman. A form of the same word was used in Genesis 22:12 when an angel of the Lord prevented Abraham from sacrificing Isaac: "Do not lay your hand on the lad, or do anything to him; for now I know that you *fear* God, since you have not withheld your son, your only son, from Me" (emphasis mine). The angel was not describing the fear of Holy Holly—an anxiety that keeps a woman or man from trusting God. Rather, this word might also be translated as "holy, reverent respect." The fear Holy Holly experiences keeps her bound, while the reverence of Abraham, of the Good Wife, does just the opposite: it frees individuals to trust God in daring ways.

A FEARLESS YES TO GOD

Although we don't always get to peek inside marriages in the Scriptures, one that we *are* privy to is the relationship between

Elizabeth and Zacharias. Zacharias was a priest. Although they'd wanted to raise children, Elizabeth and Zacharias were well past their child-bearing years. In fact, they were past the grandparenting years!

Though some have proclaimed that the only sure things in this world are death and taxes, any honest woman over seventy will tell you there are a few other things you can count on. These include graying hair, loosening skin, loss of muscle tone, and the inconvenient loss of other physical functions. Guys, don't think too long and hard about this one. By the time you've spent half a century with your beloved, she'll be more beautiful to you than she is today. What I want you to hear is that even if Elizabeth had *wanted* to, she couldn't place her hope in outward beauty.

Zecharias was fulfilling his priestly duty by burning incense in the temple when an angel appeared to him. Zecharias's remarkable encounter actually informs the way we can understand a modern Holy Holly. Zecharias had served the Lord faithfully for decades. He and Elizabeth had prayed earnestly for years that the Lord might open Elizabeth's womb. But year after year, decade after decade, there had been no baby. There had been no clear message to visit this fertility specialist or that herbal medicine guru. Yet the fact that God had not appeared to offer clear guidance or intervention had never stopped Zecharias and Elizabeth from trusting in God.

For years Elizabeth had watched all of her sisters and sisters-in-law and cousins and friends give birth. Month after month she'd wait expectantly, only to suffer disappointment after disappointment. And yet Elizabeth continued to trust in God when she did *not* receive divinely downloaded direction from the Lord.

Then one day Zecharias stumbled home from work experiencing what appeared to be a posttraumatic-stress reaction. He had at last heard from God via the angel Gabriel, who assured him Elizabeth would conceive a child in her old age. This wouldn't just be any child either. This would be the one who would turn people's hearts toward the Lord.

Pay attention to Elizabeth's reaction to this absurdly wonderful news. She didn't hire a skywriter to announce to her entire village that the Lord had spoken to her husband. She didn't purchase banner ads on Facebook to make sure all her girlfriends knew God had gotten really personal with her. Nope, instead of projecting the appearance of intimacy with God, Elizabeth simply *experienced* intimacy with God. In fact, for five months, she hid herself away (Luke 1:24). Both when her belly did not yet reveal the life inside her, and when it was getting undeniably round, Elizabeth turned her heart and face toward the Lord. What was more important to Elizabeth than communicating to others that she'd had a personal encounter with God was actually experiencing God's abiding presence with her.

HOLY MERMAID, BATMAN!

When I first met Joanne, at church, she was teaching a women's Bible study. And did that woman *know* the Word! She was a great communicator too. But although she was a talented teacher from the lectern, I didn't know how her gifting and faith in God would translate into interpersonal relationships. Would she be an exhausting and annoying Holy Holly? If I'm honest, I feared she might. Still, when Joanne invited me to a prayer group at her home, I accepted, as I'd been interested in getting to know her better.

Imagine my delight when Joanne threw open the door of her home wearing a Groucho Marx mask. The girl had game!

While the rest of us snacked and chatted before prayer, Joanne slipped away upstairs and came back down wearing a shimmering turquoise evening gown. She'd bought it for her brother's wedding and wanted to get our feedback. "Do I look like Ariel from *The Little Mermaid*?" she queried. "Tell me the truth!" So that's how I sort of fell in love with Joanne.

As I came to know her better, I discovered that Joanne was a woman who was steeped in both prayer and the Word. And, as you might guess, I was tickled to find out that she was the furthest thing in the world from Holy Holly. Joanne had a rock-solid confidence in God's goodness and presence and power in the world today. What she lacked, thankfully, were both a humorless disposition and the temptation to overspiritualize everything.

Guys, keep your eyes open for the woman who's both solidly rooted in her relationship with God and also expresses a joy and vibrancy for life.

A HUMBLE SPIRITUALITY

One of the women I most admire for her commitment to the Scriptures and deep understanding of God's Word is Gloria Copeland. She is incredibly wise and theologically solid. I truly believe that she's more aware of what God's Word says than any other female on earth right now.

When I've spent time with Gloria and her husband, Ken, I've enjoyed watching how they interact with each other, especially on the subject of the Bible. One thing I really respect about Gloria is that she listens to Ken talking for hours on the Scriptures, but she never corrects him. (She allows the Holy Spirit to do that!) And Ken will brag, "She knows the Word better than I do!" Indeed, Gloria is a woman of deep trust in God and faithfulness, but—unlike Holy Holly—she doesn't need to flaunt her knowledge of or intimacy with God. As you consider a woman to marry, let her be one who allows God to take center stage rather than *her*.

STOP, PAUSE, OR GO?

I don't want you to be confused about whether a woman who presents as being super spiritual is a Holy Holly. There are lots of women who love the Lord but don't need to advertise it.

RED FLAG 🚩

- She uses spirituality as an excuse not to act.
- She's most concerned with the appearance of righteousness.
- She's driven by a fear of the enemy.

YELLOW FLAG 🚩

- Her life is marked more by caution than by freedom.
- She's overwhelmed with thoughts about disappointing God.
- Her spirituality is joyless.

GREEN FLAG 🚩

- She pursues a private relationship with God when others aren't looking.
- She lives a life of faithful response to the Scriptures, not just waiting for God's personal invitations.
- She'll encourage you to pursue your own relationship with the Lord.

She does him good and not evil
All the days of her life.

—

Proverbs 31:12

4

TURN AWAY FROM TROPHY TINA

As I rounded the corner of the produce section and headed toward the poultry, I suddenly glimpsed my neighbor Tina across the cooler section. It looked like she was checking her reflection in the freezer-case window. I quickly dropped my eyes and carefully surveyed which chicken breasts I'd pick up for dinner.

If I studied the chicken breasts, I wouldn't have to think of a polite comment to make about Tina's new ones.

After she'd had her lips done and the veins on her legs removed, she'd told me how excited she was to have her breasts done. While I was happy enough for her, the socially appropriate remark when someone's had work done wasn't listed anywhere in Miss Manners' guide to etiquette.

"Hi, Mary," she said, strolling over.

I thought she might be proudly puffing out her chest, but that probably wasn't the case at all. Even if she'd walked over very humbly, it still would have puffed.

With a twinkle in her eye, Tina beckoned, "Well, meet the girls!" She glanced down toward her blouse.

It was sort of like she'd just given birth to twins.

Not knowing what to say to "the girls," I looked back up at Tina's face. "Well," I spitballed, "are you pleased?"

"I am," she announced. "Now Tom doesn't need to be gawking at other women."

I knew Tom, and he'd never struck me as a gawker. In fact, I'd always thought he was quite pleased that Tina was so physically attractive. He proudly posted pictures of her on Facebook, and she always seemed to be the focal point of their annual Christmas cards—surrounded by a cast of supporting actors that included two children and a few dogs. And Tom.

I wanted to respond to the gawking comment but was also unsure of the protocol. "Oh, Tina," I began. "Why would Tom need to look elsewhere? I don't really think he—"

"Stop right there!" she cut me off before I could finish. She sounded irritated. "When we were at his parents' anniversary party a few months ago, I saw him eyeing other women. He talked to his sister Jenna and her best girlfriend from back in high school for a *long* time. Don't think I didn't notice that."

"Maybe he wanted to catch up with his sister?" I queried.

She snipped, "Don't get me started on that!"

I wasn't entirely clear what I'd gotten her started on.

"He and Jenna go out to coffee every other week!" she accused. "And I know he picks up the tab too."

I still couldn't discern what the big offense was.

"Does he come by my office and invite *me* to coffee?" she asked. "No. But he makes time to grab a beer every Friday with guys from *his* office."

Though I didn't see our conversation going anywhere productive, I thought I'd make one last effort before grabbing my poultry and making a run for it.

"Maybe it would fun if you invited him out to coffee," I suggested. "What about that little coffee shop near your work?"

"So he can flirt with Brandi the barista?" she demanded, as if I should have known better than to suggest something so scandalous as mocha lattes.

Though I'd decided to move on, I couldn't *not* add, "Isn't Brandi, like, sixteen years old?" I naively thought that highlighting the fact that the bouncy barista was about four decades Tom's junior might snap Tina back to reality.

"Exactly my point!" she barked.

And that was my cue to exit.

I wanted to offer some sort of parting blessing of the breasts, but stumbled to find the right words. "Well," I affirmed, "you look great." As I said it, I tipped my eyes down to let the girls know I wasn't ignoring them.

The compliment seemed to soften her.

"Thanks," she said with genuine gratitude. "Next stop, tummy tuck!"

Though I couldn't see anything that needed to be tucked, I smiled as if the next stop on the makeover train made all the sense in the world, then grabbed a sticky cellophane-wrapped package and made my exit.

I may have also breathed a little prayer for Tom—that he would have the good sense to gawk at his wife.

TROPHY TINA

I recently saw a report on a cable news show that made me think of Tina. A man—as you might imagine—had created a graph as a warning to other men. According to his research, or at least his *opinion*, the chart illustrated his hypothesis that the more attractive a woman is, the more *nuts* she is. And while I don't feel the sweeping generalization is accurate or fair, it is an apt description of Trophy Tina.

Trophy Tina is typically a knockout. She's the kind of woman who turns heads wherever she goes. In fact, it's one of the things that her husband loved about her when they were dating. It's what he first noticed about her and—if he's honest—he'd tell you that he didn't hate the way it elevated him in the eyes of other men.

Tina's husband puts her on a pedestal. And for a while, it works for both of them. She loves the attention from him and others. He's as proud to show her off as he is of the golden golf tournament trophy he displays on the fireplace mantle. And if Tina is his trophy, in some ways he is hers as well. He's her possession, and she resents anyone who gives him attention or steals his gaze from her, since she needs constant affirmation.

Tina is highly possessive of her husband. Not only is she threatened by a casual conversation he has with a woman in the workplace cafeteria, but she even resents the attention he pays to the women in his family. She chides him for being a mama's boy. She envies his relationship with his sisters. Sometimes she even covets the time he spends with his daughter.

While Tina projects what others perceive to be an air of confidence, it's only skin deep. Tina is actually very insecure and tries to control those anxious feelings by perfecting her outward appearance. And because she's always been praised for her physical beauty, she's never accepted herself on the inside and has not developed the other parts of herself. Because so much time, energy, and money are poured into her appearance, she lives a lopsided and out-of-balance life.

Obsessed with how others perceive her, Tina never passes a reflective surface without taking a peek to make sure she'll turn heads. Sadly, her self-identity is determined by how she believes others view her. Tina does not leave her home—for anything—until she is put together: hair, make-up, jewelry, outfit, shoes, purse, jacket. If she has a bad hair day, she experiences feelings of worthlessness. And if someone comments on her attractive appearance, she believes, for a moment, that she is valuable.

In the most extreme cases, Tina will develop stalker-like behaviors. She might linger outside her husband's office at the end of the workday to see if he leaves alone. She checks her husband's texts when he steps away from his phone. She peeks into his private diary.

Everything in Tina's life is all about Tina.

A PEEK INTO THE FUTURE

Gentlemen, I wanted you to glimpse fifty-something Trophy Tina to get a look at what your future holds if you choose to marry her.

If you're dating Tina now, you probably see no problem with her beauty. I wouldn't expect you to. And please hear me: beauty is not the problem. I know plenty of attractive women who don't make everything revolve around themselves. They don't have a chronic need to be noticed. They aren't so wildly insecure that they envy their husband's mother and sisters.

I simply want you to pay attention to the way a woman behaves in relationship with others.

- Is she able to take a genuine interest in others, or does she constantly steer the conversation back to focus on herself?
- Does she say "I" more than she says "you" or "we" or "us"?
- Does she pour time and money into perfecting her appearance, or is she able to be with others when she looks more natural?
- Has she sacrificed developing important parts of herself—emotionally, socially, professionally, or spiritually—in service to her physical appearance?

Let me be blunt: when you're physically attracted to a woman, you may not recognize the warning signs. Check in with those who know you and love you—your friends, your siblings, your parents. They'll be able to tell you how they've experienced her. They'll let you know if she has taken an interest in their lives or if she's only sought attention for herself. Perhaps less clouded by her beauty, these loved ones will be better able to discern whether she wants a marriage of mutual sacrifice or if she simply wants to be adored by you and by others.

Like so many of the types I'm warning you to avoid, I want you to notice the flip side of that which you most admire about a woman. In the case of Trophy Tina, the flip side of her beauty might just be that it is given more importance than a relationship can bear.

SHE BRINGS YOU GOOD

The kind of woman who brings good to others—her husband, her family, her people—is the kind of woman described in Psalm 31.

To remind you, the author of Proverbs 31 was Solomon, the son of David and Bathsheba (also identified as one of David's favorite wives). David's rival, Saul, had been the first king of Israel; David had been the second. Solomon was its third.

I can't imagine what it would have been like to be one of David's children in a polygamous family. If scandalous cable dramas of modern polygamous families are any indicator, Solomon would have grown up knowing and relating to all of David's wives. I suppose if anyone was uniquely qualified to judge the merits of various wives, it was Solomon, who had watched six or seven function in the context of his family.

As a boy, had he paid attention to the differences between his father's wives?

Had he compared the merits of his own mother to the others?

Had he noted which wives flourished and which ones floundered?

Regardless of how he discerned it, Solomon said of the Good Wife, "She does him good and not evil / All the days of her life" (Proverbs 31:12). The Good Wife brings good to her husband and to those around her. Sadly, the trophy wife is more concerned with how she is perceived.

As you consider the type of woman you'll marry, pursue a wife who will seek the good of others—including you. While it might seem as though a marriage could work when each person pursues his or her own good, nothing could be further from the truth. Though the math looks right—two people seeking the good of two people—it never is. The healthiest and most fulfilling marriages are those in which each partner seeks the good of the other. And *others*.

A BEAUTIFUL QUEEN

The biblical countertype of the physically attractive Trophy Tina is not whom you might guess. She was not a plain or homely woman. She was a beautiful woman who was not self-serving the way Tina is. She didn't demand attention, but acted with integrity.

In Susa one year, where the Persian king Xerxes had a winter palace, two banquets were being held at the same time. One was for the king and all the men of Susa. Another was given by Queen Vashti for all the women of the royal court and the nobility. No expense was spared at these rich and exquisite royal banquets.

Things got interesting when King Xerxes got a little drunk and asked for Vashti to be brought to him. To be blunt, he wanted to show off his trophy. While Tina might have loved this, Vashti did not. Perhaps she thought she was being treated more like property, like one of the king's concubines, than with the royal respect she was due.

Vashti wasn't going to any man banquet.

Let's just say this didn't go over well with Xerxes. Still pretty tipsy, he had Vashti banished for humiliating him.

This guy needed to find another trophy wife. At the advice of his advisers—the same ones who'd convinced him to dump Vashti—the king ordered that beautiful young virgins be gathered up for makeovers, and then he'd decide who most pleased him. According to Esther 2, the nationwide search (which would have made great reality TV) was on.

I can cut to the chase and tell you that Vashti's successor was a beautiful young woman named Esther. In addition to her beauty, she was a smart cookie too. She made an alliance with one of the king's advisers that helped her win the crown.

I want you to hear how Esther used, or leveraged, her beauty.

Although Esther was Jewish, no one in the kingdom knew this. The drama got real when her uncle Mordecai refused to bow to Haman, the highest court official. Haman was furious. And not just at Mordecai, but at the Jewish people in the land. He persuaded the king that these people who were different were a threat to the kingdom, and a day was set for their slaughter.

In a most poignant twist of Shakespearean-level drama, the king who'd ordered the execution of the Jews did not realize his beloved bride was numbered among them. The tragic comedy of misunderstandings (really, read it, it's good) continued until, in response to a lavish banquet, the king offered Esther anything she desired.

With wisdom and diplomacy—knowing that it might all end poorly for her—Esther successfully lobbied for the lives of the Jewish people.

Esther's life, her esteem in the king's eyes, her royal stature—all that she might have enjoyed as a beautiful trophy wife—were leveraged for the good of the Jewish people. While Trophy Tina is all about, well, Trophy Tina, Esther had both a vision to advocate for others and the courage to execute it.

MEET THE NON-TROPHY WIFE

In 1963, a musician named Jimmy Soul released a goofy song called "If You Want to Be Happy." It's sort of the old-school version of *13 Women You Should Never Marry*. Except just one. The catchy chorus warns men not to marry a pretty woman but to search, instead, for an ugly one.

Deep, huh? I suspect Jimmy Soul may have had a bad run-in with Trophy Tina. Well, guys, I'm delighted to say that marrying a physically unattractive woman is not a requisite for a happy life.

My girlfriend Sally is a case in point. Sally is one of the most beautiful women I've ever known. Anyone who lays eyes on her would agree. But what's even more attractive than Sally's physical beauty is this: she seems to have no idea that she's drop-dead gorgeous. It's not that Sally puts herself down either. She neither deflects compliments extended to her nor goes searching for them by asking, "Do these jeans make my butt look too big?" What's actually most remarkable about Sally is that it's not evident she spends a lot of time dwelling on her appearance at all. That doesn't mean she looks like a mess, though; she takes care of herself and is cognizant of her appearance.

Pastor Tim Keller once remarked, "The essence of gospel-humility is not thinking more of myself or thinking less of myself; it is thinking of myself less."[1] Well, that's Sally! She takes such an interest in others—in her husband, in other moms on the football bleachers, in her kids' friends who are struggling in school—that she simply doesn't spend a lot of time dwelling on herself.

Gentlemen, whether a woman is physically beautiful is less important than whether her eyes are set on the welfare of others. You'll avoid marrying Trophy Tina if you set your sights on a woman whose sights are set on others.

A CONFIDENT FLESH-AND-BLOOD WOMAN

Guys, I want you to hear clearly that every beautiful woman is not a Trophy Tina. One of the most beautiful women I know, Victoria Osteen, the wife of pastor Joel Osteen, is a great example. You may be aware that he's garnered more than a little bit of attention around the globe, yet Victoria is not threatened by his success at all. Not only is she not a jealous woman, but she doesn't demand the attention of others. Victoria adores Joel and doesn't feel diminished by his success.

Gentlemen, look for a woman who can be a mutual partner with you throughout your days, not one who demands the spotlight herself.

STOP, PAUSE, OR GO?

Wouldn't it be great to know, at a glance, if a woman would behave like a Trophy Tina? Here are a few tips to identify a woman who's more concerned about the welfare of others than she is about herself.

RED FLAG

- She's envious and considers her man to be her own personal trophy.
- She's possessive of you and jealous of other women.
- She exhibits stalker-like behaviors toward you.

YELLOW FLAG

- She's overly concerned about her personal appearance.
- She can't leave home without appearing put together.
- She's envious of the legitimate other women in your life: mom, sisters, etc.

GREEN FLAG

- She takes a genuine interest in others.
- She says "you" more than "I."
- She pursues your good and the good of others.

Strength and honor are her clothing;
She shall rejoice in time to come.
—

Proverbs 31:25

5

TAKE A PASS ON PRIDEFUL PATTY

When I ran into Patty in the parking lot of a local strip mall, she behaved like I'd caught her sneaking into a strip club. She appeared visibly anxious when she caught my eye.

"Hi, Patty," I called out, waving and stepping across a grassy divider to chat as she returned to her car. "What are you up to today?"

Squirrely, like she wished we hadn't run into each other, Patty quickly stashed a few bags from Walmart into the tiny trunk of her Jaguar and slammed it shut.

"Well, I *normally* don't shop here, certainly not for clothes. But I had to pick up some school supplies for Jamie and Jenny, and since I was coming back from Saks, this was just on the way, since I had to get gas . . ."

Listening to Patty's protests was awkward. She clearly didn't realize that Walmart was both where I was headed to shop and also where I'd bought my favorite pair of jeans. When she wound down from a lengthy explanation about why she didn't shop at Walmart but *had* run several other impressive Saturday-morning errands, I inquired, "So, what were you getting at the mall?"

Even as the words came out of my mouth, I was surprised to hear them. I normally don't interrogate people about what they purchase, but I suspected that Patty would want to tell me. And, indeed, her face lit up when I asked.

"Well, Jenny was invited to a baby shower for one of her teachers at Highview Prep," she said, scooting to unlock the passenger door of her car and reaching for a large bag from a popular new designer shop for kids called Froufrou. Tuition at Highview Prep was two thousand dollars per child per month, and the twins were sophomores. Because I'd known Patty's husband, Patrick, had been out of work for about ten months, I couldn't imagine how her girls were still attending the most prestigious high school in the area. Nor why Patty didn't pick up a gift at Walmart.

I wondered whether it was a coincidence that Walmart bags got slammed into the trunk while the Froufrou one sat on display in the front seat.

Patty pulled out several cute baby outfits that I knew would fit an infant for about three weeks. She showed off a ruffly white dress trimmed in pink satin ribbon, which truly was adorable. Though I knew it would have been tacky to peek at the price tag, I had a hunch those outfits set her back a few hundred dollars.

"Isn't this darling?" she cooed. "Look, even the tag is cute!"

The store's name had been embroidered onto the canvas tag and trimmed with curly ribbon. It was true. The tag was cute. And I couldn't help but notice it had a three-digit dollar figure followed by two really cute zeroes. Had Patty meant to show me what she'd just spent on the handmade dress? I'd give her the benefit of the doubt and assume she *really* loved unique tags.

"Oh wow," I marveled, "it really is. This must be some teacher."

"Well," Patty explained, "she lives in [fancy local neighborhood], and her husband works for [prestigious company]. And not all the students were invited, so I thought it would be nice for Jenny to take something like these."

"Well, they really are cute. I think her teacher will love them."

"Oh, you know who goes to Highview now?" Patty offered. "The son of Dr. Harrison, who's the new head of oncology at the hospital. Jamie and this boy drive the same car! Isn't that funny?"

It was evident that this trivia really pleased Patty.

"And how's Patrick doing?" I asked. Don and I had been concerned about this family for the months Patrick had been unemployed.

"Oh, he's great!" she told me. "Playing *lots* of golf. Absolutely loving it. I've been thinking we should probably take a family trip down to Grenada over the girls' summer break."

Though her assurance rang hollow, I accepted it.

"That sounds nice," I agreed. "Well, please let Patrick know we send our love."

"I will," Patty promised, sliding into the driver's seat. "Great to see you, Mary."

"Take care," I replied, and turned to head into Walmart.

While I realized it didn't really matter, I secretly hoped that Patty would see me strut proudly through the entrance of the big-box retailer.

PEGGING PRIDEFUL PATTY

This Prideful Patty, as well as all the other ones out there, wanted me to know that she—as well as her husband and her daughters—was living *large*. That extravagant purchases, name-dropping, and prestigious labels weren't anything I particularly valued didn't mean anything to her.

Prideful Patty has to have the best of everything: most impressive car, name-brand clothing, biggest home in the priciest neighborhood. And, sadly, she constantly compares what she has to what others have. So it's not just about flaunting what she's got; Patty needs to have *better* stuff to flaunt than what others do. If her neighbor boasts of an eighteen-thousand-dollar entry rug, Patty will search for a twenty-thousand-dollar statue for her foyer. If a friend has a personal trainer, Patty will hire a trainer *and* a masseuse. When an acquaintance installs a backyard swimming pool, Patty gets a pool *and* a tennis court.

In case you missed it, Patty may or may not be able to afford these extravagant purchases. Embracing the reality of living within her means is less important to her than making sure she's recognized as possessing them. It doesn't matter to her that the Rolls in the driveway put their family deeper into debt or that the vacation home won't be paid off in her lifetime or her children's lifetime.

Not only does Patty boast of what she owns, but she also brags about who she claims to know. (Whether she actually does or not is of little relevance.) It's actually a little bit sad. She'll hint in every imaginable way that she is connected to this socialite, that entrepreneur, or some minor celebrity. To be connected to those with power and privilege gives her own sense of personal value a boost.

Whether Patty has a career herself or spends her husband's money, she is completely out of touch with the difference between "wants" and "needs." Although others are more able to see through it, Prideful Patty can easily convince herself that she "needs" every extravagance she purchases.

If it's difficult for you to understand the way this woman operates (and it very well may be), know simply that her identity—who she is—is wrapped up in the possession of *things*.

GLIMPSING CHRISTMAS FUTURE

Gentlemen, how do you feel when I give you this Ghost of Christmas Future glimpse of how life with Prideful Patty might unfold? If you feel nervous or concerned, my work here is done.

To knit your life together with Prideful Patty is to risk a financially and emotionally safe future. Patty will be more concerned about impressing and pleasing others—even random others to whom she's not particularly close—than about loving you.

If you're thinking that Patty sounds a bit like Trophy Tina, you're right. Both women are concerned about appearing acceptable in the eyes of others. However, where Tina is possessive of people—being both elevated as a trophy herself and tightly holding her man as her own personal prize—Patty is possessive of *things*. Although she may not even recognize it herself, Patty prizes the opinions of others, which she garners through what she owns and flaunts, above either your opinion or God's opinion.

If you're in a serious relationship right now, you might be

a bit smitten by some of the same qualities that won't seem as shiny and pretty after twenty years of marriage as they do today.

- Have you heard this woman drop names of influential people in conversations to boost her own image?
- Does she work and live within her means, or is she spending or overspending her money? Her parents' money?
- Is it important to this woman that she's seen wearing the "right" brands?

Hear me: I don't have any problem with a woman wearing or enjoying nice things. But I want to caution you to notice how much they mean to her.

Let me suggest an exercise that might shed some light on this woman. If you were to sneak into her home at night and snip off all the labels and insignias from her clothing, cut the shiny Michael Kors medallions hanging from her purses—eliminating all traces of prestige—how would she react? (Legally I'm bound to make clear that I don't recommend this. Do not try this at home!) Would the woman you love be just as happy to slip into the very same outfit that bore a fancy tag the day before as she would one without any sign of privilege? If you think she'd be fine wearing the kind of comfy knockoff jeans I love from Walmart, she might be a keeper.

And I hope that you're also learning that one of the ways to know what a woman truly values is to listen to her speech. Does the woman you love constantly compare herself to others? Does she drop names to impress others? A person's speech will often drop important clues about what she values most.

If you decide to wed a Prideful Patty, please know that keeping her happy will feel like a root canal that never ends.

CLOTHED AND LAUGHING

When Solomon describes the ideal wife, he makes no mention of elegant name-brand handbags, dinner invitations from influential or powerful people, or even whether she has a tennis court beside her swimming pool. Rather, he wrote, "Strength and honor are her clothing; / She shall rejoice in time to come" (Proverbs 31:25).

The godly Good Wife doesn't necessarily don pricey outfits but is clothed with strength and dignity. This inherent dignity and strength are found in her character, not her wardrobe or possessions.

I love the lightness Solomon described when he asserted, "She shall rejoice in time to come." In one way, both Prideful Patty and the woman Solomon described have something in common: they don't give a lot of thought to the future. But while Patty's future is certain to include a lot of debt, the Good Wife is one who trusts God—not outward appearances—for her present and her future.

STEADFAST, HUMBLE FAITHFULNESS

If Prideful Patty is obsessed with outward appearances, the biblical woman who is her holy opposite is Leah. Leah was the daughter of Laban and the older sister of Rachel. While there's much more to both Leah and Rachel, the sisters were most famously known for their relationship to Jacob. The story of these three could be fodder for a dramatic television miniseries. After Jacob stole the blessing of his father, which was rightly due to his older brother, Esau, Jacob fled to avoid being killed by Esau. When Jacob went to the well, he spotted Rachel tending the sheep of her father, Laban. It was the classic case of love at first sight. Jacob fell for Rachel, and he fell hard.

Having no idea what a catch Jacob would be—as the future father of many nations—Laban agreed to allow Jacob to marry Rachel under one condition: Jacob would work for Laban for seven years.

On the wedding night, however, that sneaky Laban pulled a fast one on Jacob, exchanging one daughter for the other. Though we're not privy to all the details of the drama, I can almost envision the switch as a cartoon-movie debacle, with Leah quietly cloaked in a veil and desperate Rachel locked away in a closet. The logic Laban offered in Genesis 29 was that it was customary for the older daughter to be given away in marriage before her sister. While this is true, I hardly think it excuses Laban's bad behavior.

Jacob and Rachel, who'd imagined their nuptials for seven years, were heartbroken. And so, when the crafty Laban offered Rachel's hand in marriage if Jacob would work seven *more* years for him, Jacob agreed. Clearly no one was eloping to Vegas back in the day.

Can you imagine what it would feel like to be Leah? A worthless pawn in Laban's selfish scheme?

Some of what we discern about Leah isn't explicit in the biblical text. Rather, it is woven between the lines. The Bible doesn't tell us if Leah was the kind of woman to speak poorly of her sister. We don't know exactly how she navigated the complicated relationship between her husband and her sibling. Remember that when Jacob married Rachel, Leah wasn't sent off to a condo in the city. She was still married to Jacob!

Leah stayed faithful to Jacob in what must have been a terribly difficult situation. But her value didn't have anything to do with outward beauty or fancy brand-name sandals. She was no ravishing beauty. Leah was a woman who remained faithful when others—namely, tragically, her husband—did *not* think highly of her.

NO NEED TO FLAUNT IT

It's important to Prideful Patty that everyone sees the kind of status symbols that would (in her own mind) make her appear valuable and worth knowing: a flashy car, a custom home, designer labels, kids in prestigious schools. But her opposite, as I've learned from my friend Janelle, is *not* Pathetic Penelope. It's not someone who's ashamed that she can't afford the car, the home, the threads, or the schools. (I'd caution you to avoid this Penelope gal as well.)

Janelle has been very successful in the business world. She's a savvy entrepreneur who's built a company helping individuals and families who face a transition from the home they've lived in into assisted living or other more modest living situations. And though Janelle has the resources to behave like Prideful Patty—actually, probably more—she consistently makes choices that do not flaunt her wealth or status. It really boils down to more than a matter of dollars and cents. Janelle is so solidly grounded in her identity as a beloved child of God that the perceptions of others are essentially irrelevant to her.

Doesn't this sound like a fabulous way to live?

What's remarkable is that others so easily perceive this about Janelle. They recognize the freedom she experiences as a woman whose identity is secure in the Lord. In fact, Janelle's freedom—to wear secondhand clothing, to drive the same car for almost two decades, or to live in a home that's not extravagant—liberates other women around her. She is truly a gift.

Men, be sure to keep your eyes open for the woman whose identity does not depend on outward appearances. Trust me, you will be blessed by her.

NOT TOO PROUD TO SHOP SMART

Patty's opposite, one of the most humble people I know, is Lindsay Roberts. When Lindsay was in law school, she married Richard Roberts, the son of Oral Roberts. Whether due to her own achievements or those of her husband or father-in-law, Lindsay might very easily have become like Prideful Patty. Yet Lindsay has always been a godly woman, unconcerned with others' opinions of her. She admits she shops at a vintage consignment store—something Prideful Patty would never do! During some of the rough patches Lindsay has endured, Prideful Patty would have bolted, concerned about her image. But Lindsay has never been driven by others' opinions of her.

STOP, PAUSE, OR GO?

Unfortunately, no Prideful Patty will telegraph her identity by wearing a monogrammed sweater announcing "P. P." Rather, you need to pay attention to more subtle cues about the facade Patty presents to the world.

RED FLAG 🚩

- She presents to others the appearance that she's more than she is.
- She spends more than she has to impress others.
- She constantly compares herself to others.

YELLOW FLAG 🚩

- She name-drops to let you know she's well connected.
- She can't distinguish wants from needs.
- She hides, or covers up, that which (in her mind) doesn't impress.

GREEN FLAG 🚩

- She doesn't take herself too seriously.
- Her sense of identity is rooted firmly in the Lord rather than outward appearances.
- She can roll with off-brand products!

Her husband is known in the gates,
When he sits among the elders of the land.

—

Proverbs 31:23

6

CHASE AWAY CRITICAL CATHY

Sipping a cup of coffee at my laptop, I couldn't believe what I was reading on Facebook. It was the stuff of middle school drama.

Along with a picture of an overgrown lawn, Cathy had posted, "Look at this mess. He had a 'business' trip to Hawaii all week. The weekend is almost over, and guess who hasn't mowed the lawn!"

Unfortunately, it was obvious to me—and to the hundreds of others who'd read the childish accusation—that Cathy was dissing her husband on social media.

I felt my gut tighten with tension.

Cathy and her husband had been limping along like this

for as long as I'd known them. But it wasn't just her husband Cathy had problems with. It was *everyone*.

About three years ago a friend confided in me about a painful encounter with Cathy. She and Cathy had known each other since childhood. And while Melissa had learned over the years not to share her most intimate matters with Cathy, she'd learned it the hard way. In tears, Melissa shared that in the context of a women's small group, Cathy had revealed Melissa had had an abortion when she was in high school.

All I could do was hold Melissa while she wept. I knew she'd experienced forgiveness and redemption for her past, but I also recognized that Cathy had violated her friend's trust by revealing something so deeply personal.

Unfortunately, I'd also seen Cathy behave this way in relation to her children. Rather than protecting their hearts, she'd leave them vulnerable and exposed in public. At a school basketball game, Cathy called out to her son on the bench, "So, did she tell you why she dumped you?" His face revealed that he was mortified.

I'd also been shocked by Cathy's Facebook content when she posted her daughter had gotten her period for the first time and that that probably explained why she'd been so moody for months. Curious, and concerned about her daughter's heart, I'd scrolled through Cathy's friends list to see if her post would end up on her daughter's news feed.

I guess I wasn't surprised when I discovered they weren't Facebook friends. Being "friends" with Cathy—in life or in cyber life—was risky business.

As I glanced back at the picture of Cathy and Chuck's overgrown yard, I remembered an encounter we'd had at their home. She'd invited us to dinner at seven. Chuck's flight had been due to land at six but had been delayed. We were all enjoying appetizers in the living room when he barreled through the door. Leaving his suitcase and briefcase in the front hall, he rushed in apologetically to greet us.

"You're not going to leave that mess there, are you?" Cathy demanded.

"I just wanted to say hello to Don and Mary," he explained. His tone sounded more like that of a child who'd just been scolded than of a man.

As you might expect, it felt very awkward.

As he left the room to put his travel gear away, Cathy continued, "He acts like he lives in a barn! I swear, I even find messes when he's gone. Some days I think my life would just be easier if he'd stay on these trips instead of coming home."

I pressed my lips together to keep from saying what I was thinking: *I'll bet Chuck has had the same thought.*

When Chuck returned, Cathy griped about the food getting cold—which struck me as odd since the soup she'd prepared was actually still simmering on the stove—and grumped around as she put it out on the table.

I wish I could say that our conversation during the meal was an improvement over the way the visit had begun. But that would be lying. Cathy laid into her pastor because she'd disagreed with his Sunday sermon. She criticized Chuck's mother. She complained to Don about her doctor's bedside manner. Basically, she "stirred the pot." (And I don't mean the delicious vat of soup.)

As Don and I drove home, I saw a picture of Chuck in my mind's eye. In my imagination I saw his face and body covered with bruises. I don't know how he manages, but I suspect he tries to make the best of a difficult situation for his children.

CRITICAL CATHY

Have you ever known anyone like this hypercritical Cathy? Have you ever wished you didn't?

Cathy causes strife and trouble wherever she goes. Tragically, she's miserable if everyone else is happy and only really seems content when she's made everyone else miserable too. Something about this seems to soothe her. But although it works for her, those around her are left bruised and battered.

Cathy is an adrenaline addict. While it would probably be safer and healthier for everyone if she began bungee jumping off of bridges, she is fueled by interpersonal conflict. And because she's not able to sustain meaningful lasting friendships, she causes conflict wherever she can find it: with strangers driving in traffic, in the front office of her daughter's high school, at the checkout line at the grocery store. Easily offended, Cathy seems to get into it with people wherever she goes.

Critical Cathy views herself as a victim of others. Her general attitude says, *If it weren't for bad luck, I'd have none at all.* As Don would say, she has a negative mental filter toward life. It's almost as if she were wearing glasses that cloud whatever she sees. Unable to recognize the good in others, she focuses only on the bad. And when good comes her way? Those cloudy glasses go completely dark. Cathy can find something wrong with even the most generous blessings she receives.

Cathy seems to have no awareness that family members protect one another. Just as a husband covers, or protects, his wife, so, too, a wife is made to protect her husband and her children. Yet Cathy's behavior leaves her loved ones feeling vulnerable and exposed.

As you've probably figured out, Cathy is not the person to trust as a confidante. She will wield the most personal information as a weapon to create conflict. She will complain to her girlfriends about what happens between her and her husband in the bedroom. She'll grump to your family about matters between the two of you. She'll share details about her children's lives, which they'd rather keep private, with friends and acquaintances.

Can you imagine one day being the father of children who don't trust their mother? It is absolutely heartbreaking.

DON'T DISMISS HER TOO QUICKLY

Perhaps as you read about this nightmare on wheels you wondered, *Who would ever choose someone like that to marry? I know I wouldn't!*

News flash: no one ever thinks they've chosen the wrong person.

If you're a guy who's a bit shy or withdrawn, you could be naturally attracted to someone like Cathy. In the beginning you might admire her ability to vocalize her thoughts. You like the way she sticks up for herself. Because she's never at a loss for something to say, she might even seem to make your life a bit more comfortable. And yet, like so many of the types I want to caution you against, that which attracts you has a negative flip side I desperately want you to see.

While Cathy's vocal nature might seem fresh or intriguing while you're dating, imagine how it could express itself fifteen or twenty years in the future. As you think about building your family, try to extrapolate into the future how Critical Cathy's behavior will impact you and the ones you love. Besides being a thorn in *your* flesh, Cathy will never earn the trust that will allow her to nurture the hearts of your children. Although it seems odd to consider at this point, trust me when I tell you that to avoid Critical Cathy now is to protect children who aren't even yet born!

Where there is no strife, Cathy will create it. She'll be critical of your friends. She'll complain about your parents. She'll drive a wedge between you and your siblings. She'll criticize the way you do your job and the ways she feels you don't do your job. She'll complain when you're away, and when you return she'll find something else to harp on.

Like anyone, expect Cathy to be on her best behavior if you're dating her. (Let's be honest: it's what we all do.) I encourage you to pay attention to your gut. When she jumps on you for being five minutes late or nags about the way you keep your car, do you notice any warning signals—a tightness or anxious pulsing inside—that all is not well? If Cathy doesn't have many girlfriends, are you willing to confront the reasons for that?

Five or ten or twenty years from now is not the time to open your eyes to the truth and be honest with yourself about this woman. It's *now*.

SHE BUILDS UP HER HUSBAND

While Critical Cathy spews words that destroy, the Good Wife offers words that bring life—especially the words she speaks to her husband and about her husband. The godly

Good Wife uses her words to encourage and build up her groom. Among those who extend respect and honor to her husband, she is first in line. King Solomon said of the faithful and Good Wife, "Her husband is known in the gates, / When he sits among the elders of the land" (Proverbs 31:23).

Gentlemen, this is the gal you want to marry!

Contrast the way the Good Wife honors and respects her husband with the way Critical Cathy tears hers down. Throughout Proverbs, Solomon both warned of the wicked tongue and exalted the one that speaks with wisdom and grace. Proverbs 4:24, a father's instruction to his son, warns, "Put away from you a deceitful mouth, / And put perverse lips far from you." Solomon knew that words matter. By avoiding poisonous speech, we protect those around us.

Solomon also gave a plug for speech that is full of grace. In Proverbs 22:11, he advised, "He who loves purity of heart / And has grace on his lips, / The king will be his friend." Throughout the Old Testament and New Testament Scriptures there's an intimate connection between the heart that is pure and good and what flows forth from the lips. The godly woman has a pure heart that speaks gracious words to build up and not tear down.

As you consider the woman you'd like to marry, do you find she is a woman who will respect you, just as you respect her? Does she give evidence of that respect in her speech?

The type of woman you should aim to marry is the kind

about whom people remark, "I've never heard her say a bad word about anyone." The godly woman who encourages others with her speech, the one who wears gracious spectacles that recognize the good in others, the one who speaks forth wisdom, is one who will extend to you the same respect with her words and her actions.

THE SISTER WHO HELD HER TONGUE

Critical Cathy creates strife not just with her husband but in all her relationships. If there's one woman in the Bible we might expect to behave like Critical Cathy—stirring up dissent, causing strife—it would be Rachel.

As we read earlier, when Rachel and Jacob spotted each other at the well—she a shepherdess, tending to her sheep, and he on a journey—it was love at first sight. When Jacob met Rachel's father, Laban, he suggested a deal: "I will serve you seven years for Rachel your younger daughter" (Genesis 29:18).

Seven years this guy worked for the privilege of marrying the love of his life. And yet as we read, on the night of the wedding, Laban pulled a fast one on Jacob, giving Jacob his *older* daughter, Leah. While this might have worked out great for Laban—who swindled Jacob into another seven years of labor—it's hard to imagine that Jacob, Rachel, or Leah could have been very thrilled with the awkward arrangement. Jacob and Rachel did marry, seven years later, and the three continued to remain as family to one another throughout their lives.

If anyone could have benefited from talking trash about someone else, it would seem to be Rachel. She could have torn down Leah with her speech the way Critical Cathy lays into her husband, tearing him down. But Rachel held her tongue. For fourteen years she waited to marry Jacob, and then she waited many more years—while Leah was having child after child—to bear his sons.

Yes, Rachel might have trash-talked her sister, Leah (aka "the competition"), and she also would have had ample opportunity to bad-mouth Jacob. But even in the most difficult circumstances, Rachel continued to honor both of them.

NEVER AN ILL WORD

I once heard my Critical Cathy friend badger another woman who happened to be holding her tongue while several women around her gossiped.

"You've never said a bad word about anyone!" While some women might have extended the words gently, as a compliment, on Cathy's razor-sharp tongue they sounded more like an accusation.

Guys, keep your ears open for the woman who could be accused of the same.

I've known Margie for about fifteen years. She's a marriage and family therapist, and she also guides others as a spiritual director. The reason both of these are such a natural and perfect fit for Margie is that people *trust* her. Though I've of course not been privy to these privileged relationships, I've seen the way our friends are able to share their hard stories with Margie, and I've noticed the way she holds them in confidence as treasures that don't belong to her. I have every reason to believe that she's handled my private story with the same delicate care. Never once have I heard Margie utter one inappropriate word about anyone. She truly sees the very best in every individual. It's almost as if God has given her the same kind of X-ray vision power He uses to see the person He made each individual to be. That's how Margie sees!

Guys, listen for the words a woman speaks about others, and notice whether she's generous or hypercritical and if she's able to protect people with her words rather than expose them.

MARIA "THE VAULT"

As a pastor at Christ Tabernacle, the first church that came out of Brooklyn Tabernacle, Maria Durso has—like so many pastors' wives—been privy to lots of information. Yet I have never once heard Maria expose others' pain or hurt. She not only protects others' secrets, but Maria would never judge anyone. Maria is able to recognize what is valuable and good and precious about others.

No stranger to pain herself, Maria has a heart that's tender and sensitive to those who are experiencing difficulties. She's an incredible support to her husband and blessing to her sons. Guys, notice how the woman you're considering marrying speaks about others. Does she protect with her words, or, like Critical Cathy, does she use them to tear down and destroy?

STOP, PAUSE, OR GO?

With her speech, Critical Cathy trashes others. Because words have the power to tear down and the power to build up, employ an attentive ear to notice which type the woman you love is when speaking to others and about others.

RED FLAG 🚩

- She publicly shames those closest to her.
- She exposes secrets entrusted to her.
- She is hypercritical of others.

YELLOW FLAG 🚩

- She stirs the pot to draw others into arguments.
- She's easily offended.
- She views the world with a negative mental filter.

GREEN FLAG 🚩

- She protects people emotionally.
- She has a circle of friends who trust her.
- She doesn't speak unkindly about anyone.

She watches over the ways of her household,
And does not eat the bread of idleness.

—

Proverbs 31:27

7

AVOID ADDICTED ANNIE

Someone had pulled out the karaoke machine at our neighborhood Christmas party and my neighbor Annie—who was, we'll say, "well lubricated"—was belting out a song of woe. Glittering in a short black holiday dress, slurring some of the lyrics, she continued to croon one of those "somebody done somebody wrong" songs.

On one hand, any drunken reveler might have belted out the same chorus. But something about the words Annie had chosen to sing sounded as if they were drifting straight up and out of her deep places.

I'd known Annie for about eight years. She stayed at home with her children and served as a volunteer at the local library. The previous year she'd spent several summer months in a recovery center, but now she was clearly drinking again.

Our lives had overlapped for a season when we joined forces to carpool our boys to school and sporting events. It's funny: in my memories of hauling bats and balls out of her trunk, there were always about four or five crisp new shopping bags—from Macy's, Nordstrom, Saks—full of lavish purchases.

We also spent time sitting together in the bleachers, where I'd watch the game and she'd rant about one thing or another. A typical example was her reaction to a visit from her folks—Annie went on and on about how horrible they were. Her mother, she accused, filled her refrigerator with groceries without permission. Her father, unauthorized, cleaned out her garage. And while I struggled to identify what was so criminal about their behavior, Annie seethed with rage toward them.

When something went wrong with her marriage (always her husband's fault, never hers), Annie would point to some parenting omission or commission from her childhood. It actually became like an odd game for me: no matter what had raised her ire during the day, I knew that someone else would be blamed. About one-third of the time it was her mother. One-third of the time it was her husband. And the other third fell to the rest of the planet.

Though I'd always understood, intellectually, that people who feel a void in their lives will be tempted to fill it with other things, I'd never seen it lived out like I did with my neighbor. By five o'clock each evening she had a cocktail in her hand. She filled her closets with piles of clothes, some she never even wore. She'd fill her mouth with the most delicious of foods, and the next day she'd nearly kill herself trying to work off the calories.

As a mom, it was hard to see the way Annie's unhealed hurts impacted her children. Yes, they'd lost their mom the previous summer during her time in rehab. But more than that, I knew she was emotionally absent every single evening. They needed her to see them, but Annie really only had eyes for Annie.

I could recognize that Annie had endured some real challenges during her childhood. Her parents had remained married, but they had a volatile relationship. Both of them had physically abused Annie when she was young. Over the years I'd seen other women with similar stories find healing and freedom as they encountered the radical and transforming love of Christ. Not Annie. Although she attended church, she had not yet been set free from all that bound her.

As Annie's off-key ballad of woe wound down, her husband gently eased her off the stage. "Come on, Ann. Time to go home," he coaxed in a soothing tone. This wasn't the first time he'd had to guide her toward safe slumber.

"But somebody done me wrong!" Annie insisted.

Her groom cooed, "I know, I know."

ADDICTED ANNIE

If you've ever met someone like Annie, you know that she spends a lot of time looking in the rearview mirror of life. To anyone who's willing to listen, Annie will rehash the losses she's endured throughout her lifetime. The word that might best describe Addicted Annie is *stuck*. *Stuck* means that she's not been able to heal from the past and move on to experience meaning and fulfillment in the present. Sadly, her present—and therefore the present of her husband and children and other loved ones—is riddled with disappointments and hurts from the past.

Although Addicted Annie may have had periods of sobriety—especially during courtship—she's never experienced true freedom from her addiction. She has not successfully weathered difficult seasons while remaining sober. She hasn't developed practices that ground her in her new identity. She's not invited others toward the road to recovery. She's not accompanied others on their journeys to wholeness.

The more predictable pattern in Annie's life is that, averse to pain, she fills herself with whatever promises to soothe the deep ache inside. Sometimes she uses alcohol. Other times she turns to food. She may abuse prescription medication. She may shop till she drops. (Or at least until her credit rating does.) She may turn to men outside of her marriage in an attempt to fill the void.

While plenty of individuals have faced some of the same challenges Annie has—growing up in homes with addiction, violence, and chaos—not all have remained stuck as Annie has. Rather, the individuals who find freedom are those who've experienced the deep, deep love of Jesus and have been transformed and set free by that love. There's nothing rote or falsely religious about these folks. If you find a woman who's been saturated by Christ's great redeeming love for her and for the world, hang on to her!

YOU CAN'T ALWAYS RECOGNIZE AN ADDICT BY THE TRACK MARKS ON HER ARM

I want to be very clear about the kind of woman I'm describing in Addicted Annie. I'm not detailing a woman who's had moments of poor judgment. I'm not talking about a woman with a few failures in her past. I'm describing a person who has repeated and repeated and repeated this pattern of self-soothing behavior.

There are women who've endured very difficult circumstances but have done the emotional and spiritual work they needed to do to become healthy people and great wives. There are women who've truly conquered their addictions and will remain sober for the rest of their days. I want to be clear that God has the power to redeem the most compromised lives.

The Addicted Annie I want to warn you about is the one who's been unable or unwilling to truly deal with her past. Rather than accepting the hard work of grief and forgiveness and healing, Annie has stuffed down her pain. She's walled it away. And, hidden from the healing power of light and air, her deepest wounds have continued to fester rather than heal.

I happen to know that this particular Annie I've mentioned had an eighteen-month period of sobriety in the time leading up to her wedding. Her fiancé knew that she'd wrestled with addiction but assumed that because she wasn't drinking she had conquered it. But "not drinking" isn't the same thing as redemptive transformation.

What I want you to hear from me are the words I'd want to share with my grandsons if they brought home a girl who was still in the process of redemption: "Be careful." I'd want them to know that, like walking barefoot in a parking lot, they need to be extra cautious to keep from being hurt.

I'd also want to say, "I can understand some of the reasons you're attracted to Annie." If you struggle, or have struggled, with your own addictions, Annie might make you feel better about yourself. Or if you're a rescuer, you may notice the impulse to help Annie get her life together. I can't stress how important it is, as you consider the wife God will give you, to pay attention to what's at work inside of you.

Remember the story of Shadrach, Meshach, and

Abednego? The Bible reports that when these three guys, who'd been thrown into the fiery furnace, stepped out of the flames, they didn't even smell of smoke. So as you consider the big-picture view of a woman, understand that although your eyes and your ears will give you some information, so will your nose! Do you recognize the fragrant air of the Holy Spirit? Or does the smell of stale smoke—tobacco? pot? meth?—continue to linger in the life of this woman?

Guys, your mission is to find a helpmate, not a mate to help. If you're serious enough to consider marriage, practice due diligence by not only staying alert to the signals Annie might be sending to you, but also knowing it's fair game to ask those close to Annie who will tell you the truth about the way she lives her life.

SHE AVOIDS BREAD THAT DOES NOT SATISFY

Though Solomon didn't mention food addiction, alcohol dependency, or pill popping, he did describe the Good Wife as one who cares for those around her. He reported, "She watches over the ways of her household, / And does not eat the bread of idleness" (Proverbs 31:27).

Because Addicted Annie is thoroughly consumed with herself—her wounds, their enduring effect, and how she can soothe them daily—she's not able to live in the present with the people God has given her to love and to serve, namely her husband and her children. When her energy and resources are invested in keeping pain at bay, rather than living a fruitful life of love, she is in effect idle. When she numbs her feelings, she also numbs her ability to do what God has called her to do. The eyes God made to watch over the affairs of her household, her relationships, her career are focused solely on herself.

Rather than take herself out of the game, Solomon taught, the Good Wife is one who's attentive to those around her. Because she's running on a full tank, having experienced God's redemptive love for herself, she's able to care for others and be fruitful and productive.

THE MOST UNLIKELY CONVERSATION

One of the most intriguing women in Scripture is one Jesus met beside a well. Her story is recorded in the fourth chapter of John's gospel. Everything about this story is odd:

- She was a woman, which means she typically wouldn't be speaking to a rabbi.
- She was a Samaritan, a race who despised the Jews and were typically despised in return.
- She was a disreputable sinner.

Jesus' disciples had gone to the supermarket to grab some lunch when He struck up this unlikely conversation. She was clearly surprised He even acknowledged her. But when

He did, the conversation moved quickly from skimming the top of the well water to plummeting to the depths of this woman's heart.

When Jesus asked her for a drink, the woman reminded Jesus that it was nutty He was even addressing her.

In a beautiful poetic speech—that just about no one would have understood—Jesus announced, "If you knew the gift of God, and who it is who says to you, 'Give Me a drink,' you would have asked Him, and He would have given you living water" (John 4:10).

This Samaritan woman naturally thought He was talking about physical water. So she said, "I'm in! Tell me where to find it!" As their encounter continued to unfold, she came to recognize Jesus as the One who would change the world.

Though we're not privy to how this woman's life unfolded, we can trust Jesus' assurance, "Whoever drinks of this water will thirst again, but whoever drinks of the water that I shall give him will never thirst. But the water that I shall give him will become in him a fountain of water springing up into everlasting life" (John 4:13–14). This woman had been shunned by her community and yet was received by Jesus. When she was, that deep hole in her heart, the well shaft that simply could not be filled by a series of men, was at last overflowing. That's what Jesus meant when He promised that whoever drank living water wouldn't be thirsty again. I am confident that if we could glimpse this woman after she encountered Jesus, not only would she no longer be with men who used and abused her, but she'd also not have replaced men with any other substitute meant to soothe her deep hurts. She would be healed, from the inside out, with the living water that truly satisfies.

SHE MIGHT HAVE BEEN AN ANNIE

Addicted Annie believes that "somebody done her wrong," and she looks for love and comfort in all the wrong places. Yes, basically, she's a country-and-western song gone wrong.

If you could see the first twenty years of my friend Jessica's life, the trajectory might suggest she was on her way to becoming a lot like Annie. Jessica's father left their family when she was six, and her mother worked two jobs to care for Jessica and her two sisters. As a teen, Jessica was in a brutal car accident, and while she was recovering in the hospital, her mother died suddenly of a brain aneurism. Although an aunt came to live with them, at sixteen Jessica basically began raising her two younger sisters. At the time Jessica had a boyfriend who'd been offering her pot. But when her life turned upside down, she broke up with her boyfriend and focused on caring for her sisters.

If anybody had a right to sing a "somebody done somebody wrong" song, it would be Jessica. But not only did she not turn to alcohol or drugs or food or sex for comfort, she didn't spend a moment feeling sorry for herself. Instead, during that chaotic time in her life, Jessica rooted herself in the promises of God she so desperately needed. Today, forty years later, Jessica is a successful businesswoman and a happily married mother of two and grandmother of three. And let me tell you, she is a true blessing to her husband, Scott. When life gets hard—which it invariably does—Jessica is a rock of strength for Scott and for others who suffer. Though she might very understandably have made the choices Addicted Annie has made, Jessica has turned instead to drink at the well of living water.

DRINKING FROM THE WELL THAT TRULY SATISFIES

One woman I know, whom I'll call Marla, is married to a high-profile husband, the head of a well-known parachurch ministry. They're both in their early thirties. Most people can't begin to imagine the kind of demands that are placed on a couple in this kind of spotlight, not to mention the constant barrage of criticism that comes their way. It would be easily imaginable that someone facing these pressures could turn to false substitutes to comfort or satisfy themselves. Many do. But Marla, who's keenly aware of these stresses, has navigated some of the pressures in wonderfully creative ways. Refusing to comfort herself with what does not satisfy, Marla exercises regularly, power walking with girlfriends, to relieve stress. She's also part of a small group of other women facing similar challenges that meets and prays together once a month. Moment by moment, day by day, she consistently rejects the kinds of substitutes—food, alcohol, entertainment, shopping, pills, and others—that do not satisfy. Marla is a godly woman who turns to God to meet the deep needs of her heart.

STOP, PAUSE, OR GO?

Though Addicted Annie might not be a crack-smoking addict, she does have a habit of turning for comfort to that which does not satisfy. Whether it's food or pills or liquor or sex, the hole in her heart won't be filled by cheap substitutes.

RED FLAG

- She turns to substances to comfort herself.
- She believes the world is against her.
- She's not able to be present with others.

YELLOW FLAG

- She has childhood hurts she isn't willing to deal with.
- She blames others for her troubles.
- She frequently recounts her life's losses.

GREEN FLAG

- She's bravely faced the hurts of the past.
- She has truly experienced the Lord's redemptive touch.
- She refuses to find comfort outside of that which the Lord offers.

She considers a field and buys it;
From her profits she plants a vineyard.

—

Proverbs 31:16

8

BACK AWAY FROM BROKE BETSY

I was on a flight approaching Houston when the glowing screens on the seatbacks went dim. A few people looked up. Some reached into their bags for an iPad or other device to switch on when their rerun of the *Seinfeld* show faded to black.

In his most friendly, trusted, and "helpful" voice, the flight attendant began to describe what sounded like manna from heaven: the Patriot Airlines Rewards-Plus VIP Gold Card. This card, he told us, would give us airline tickets and car rental discounts and somehow would even magically put gas in the tanks of those rentals. Truly, he made it sound like when we spent ten dollars they'd give us twenty in return.

At least that's what the young woman sitting next to me heard.

Betsy, whom I'd chatted with on the flight, remarked, "That sounds awesome, right? It's like they're *paying* you to shop!"

"Well," I began, "it's not quite—"

"I'm in!" Betsy interrupted. "That annual Bosom Buddy pass means when I get married next fall we'll have a free honeymoon in the Caribbean!"

"Well, it's not exactly a 'free' trip," I began again before I was interrupted once more.

"And since I'll get the pass each year, we could have each anniversary on the same island!"

Betsy was really on a roll now.

"Are you getting one?" she asked, as if they were handing out small foil bags of free peanuts.

I explained to Betsy that I wasn't in the market for a credit card. What I *wanted* to say was that it didn't seem like she should be either. I guessed Betsy was about twenty-one or twenty-two.

"Have you *had* a credit card before?" I queried.

"Lots!" she confirmed proudly, pulling a yellow leather wallet out of her purse to show me a bulging stack. "A girl's gotta shop. Am I right? I do love me some shoes."

"Oh dear." I held in a gasp and queried, "And are you able to pay all those off?"

"Well," she explained, "not the *whole* amount. But most months I'm able to pay *something*. I work part-time at a hotel. And after I graduate from school, get a job, and get married, they're going to give me some more hours."

The flight attendant was now about three rows in front of us, handing out credit card applications. I thought I might have seen Betsy shiver a little bit. Though I probably should have bitten my tongue, I had to ask, "Is your fiancé okay with the cards and the debt?"

"He never asked. I guess he'll find out soon enough!" she quipped. "When we land, I can't wait to tell him about the Bosom Buddy passes."

The word *debt* seemed to have no more meaning for Betsy than if I'd uttered it in Mandarin. She seemed truly oblivious. I started thinking about her poor fiancé. If I saw this unsuspecting guy at baggage claim, I knew I'd be tempted to pull him aside and issue a stern warning. It was probably best for Betsy that I only had a carry-on.

"And what kind of work does your fiancé do?" I inquired.

"Well," Betsy began, "right now he caddies at a golf course, but after graduation he wants to find a job as a history teacher. And I know there are a lot of school districts that are just desperate for teachers. So I don't think it should be too hard."

The flight attendant reached across me to extend a credit card application to Betsy. She'd already pulled a fancy engraved Gucci pen out of her bag. (Who even knew they made pens?)

The mama in me wanted to protect Betsy from herself. "Betsy, are you sure this is a good idea?" I queried gently.

"Oh, it's a great idea!" she chirped. "You heard him say what you get, right? This is *awesome*."

I decided to let it rest.

UNFORTUNATELY, BROKE'S NOT A JOKE

It's not just that Betsy is broke. Being broke can have its own inherent dignity. When people struggle financially and choose not to accrue debt for wants and whims, "broke" has an awful lot of integrity.

Broke Betsy, though, has maxed out her credit cards. She has sixty pairs of shoes. Rather than finding new homes for any of them, she jokes that she'll just buy a new closet. A retailer's dream, Betsy is constantly at the mall, at T.J. Maxx, at Marshalls, searching for the next new thing. (And once some of these new things make it home, some never even leave her overcrowded closet.)

For Betsy, spending money has become a habit. It gives her a rush. And sadly, she has lost all perspective about the difference between "wants" and "needs." If she's invited to go line dancing, she convinces herself she needs six-hundred-dollar cowboy boots from Barneys. Or a limited-edition, hand-finished cowgirl hat that sets her back $250. She's lost all perspective to recognize that not every want is actually a need.

Betsy does not yet see the light. She doesn't recognize what is so very problematic about her habits.

FIND OUT NOW, NOT LATER

Gentlemen, if you're in a relationship with a woman and don't know what her financial situation is like, I hope you've begun to wonder. If you're curious enough to initiate this sometimes sensitive conversation with the woman in your life, my work is done.

Unless you believe her when she tells you that the forty-five-thousand-dollar debt isn't a big deal. And that everyone has debt. And to just lighten up. In that case, my work is not done. Neither is yours.

I cannot stress this enough: proceed with caution. Walk slowly. If Betsy spends her money—or her credit—so freely, it will be twice as easy for her to spend when your income is added to the shared pot. If Betsy cannot keep her word with her debtors, how will she keep her word with you?

Like so many of these sticky areas, the flip side of careless spending might be one of the reasons you were attracted to Betsy in the first place. Does she drive a nice car? Have high-end appliances in her apartment? Does she dress to impress? (You might not be impressed by the designer tags, but trust me when I tell you that other women are.)

If there's someone special in your life right now, I encourage you to have a frank conversation about money. And this goes both ways; if you've accrued inordinate debt, make sure you come clean too. How many credit cards do you each use? Have you maxed them out? What other debt will each of you bring into a marriage?

In addition to the financial facts, begin to notice some other clues that Betsy might be in trouble. Does she constantly call Daddy for money? Does she need loans from siblings? If Betsy works a steady job and continues to be in the hole, know you need to investigate a little bit further.

Up until now, your money has been your money and Betsy's money has been Betsy's money. Guess what? When you marry, Betsy's debt becomes your debt. And, honestly, the current debt might not even be the worst of it. What could be a larger burden to your marriage are the habits Betsy has allowed to develop. If she assures you she'll "be more careful," but you've seen no evidence of the fact, exercise extreme caution.

Although no one really ever knows exactly what they're saying when they promise to remain faithful "for better or for worse," mounting personal debt is going to make "worse" come sooner rather than later. Did you know that financial strain on a marriage is the number one cause for divorce? Cited more often than infidelity, financial stress destroys marriages. If you marry Broke Betsy, you're setting yourself up for failure.

THE RESPONSIBLE STEWARD OF MONEY

Solomon didn't mention the industry and financial savvy of the Good Wife once. Or twice. Or even three times. It could be argued that at least *half* of Solomon's description of the Good Wife details a woman who's financially savvy. (He must have known about the grim divorce statistics.) In case you missed it, gentlemen, the Good Wife is the anti-Betsy!

Notice in Proverbs 31 where Solomon describes about a woman who's financially responsible and hardworking:

- "She seeks wool and flax, / And willingly works with her hands" (v. 13).
- "She also rises while it is yet night, / And provides food for her household, / And a portion for her maidservants" (v. 15).
- "She considers a field and buys it; / From her profits she plants a vineyard" (v. 16).
- "She girds herself with strength, / And strengthens her arms" (v. 17).
- "She perceives that her merchandise is good, / And her lamp does not go out by night" (v. 18).
- "She stretches out her hands to the distaff, / And her hand holds the spindle" (v. 19).

- "She makes linen garments and sells them, / And supplies sashes for the merchants" (v. 24).
- "She watches over the ways of her household, / And does not eat the bread of idleness" (v. 27).
- "Give her of the fruit of her hands, / And let her own works praise her in the gates" (v. 31).

Had Solomon described the Good Wife today, in the twenty-first century, he might have said:

This woman burns the candle at both ends. Instead of lounging at the spa getting a mani-pedi, or compulsively shopping every week at Ross, she's investing in a rental property that will produce additional income for her family. She's one smart financial cookie, this lady. Bills? Paperwork? She's on top of them. Her husband notices it and others do too. This woman's a keeper, guys. If you find her, hang on to her.

BEST. JOB. EVER.

In my opinion, one of the most interesting professions in the Bible is that of Lydia. This woman from Thyatira was "a seller of purple [cloth]" (Acts 16:14). While the only color-specific dealers I'm aware of nowadays are those who specialize in college and pro sports—think of Orlando Magic's bright blue or

Clemson University's vivid orange—back in the first century, dealing in purple was a legitimate business enterprise. In fact, not only was Thyatira known for purple, but the waters there were renowned for aiding in the production of gorgeous scarlet fabrics.

Lydia had it going on. In an age before credit card debt made it possible for many, she owned an impressive home and employed a number of servants.

Paul and others first encountered Lydia by the riverside where she was dying cloth alongside other women. (Which sounds so much more fun than doing tie-dye alone at home in the washing machine.) Luke wrote that Lydia was a person who worshiped God, but she wasn't yet a Christian. When she joyfully received Paul's message of grace, which led to her baptism and subsequently the baptism of her entire household, Lydia turned her life over to Jesus Christ. In fact, today Lydia is recognized as the first European convert to Christianity.

We glimpse that Lydia opened her home to extend hospitality to the missionaries God had sent. Later, when Paul and Silas were released from prison, she welcomed them into her home as well. Not only was she a savvy businesswoman, responsible with her money, but she was willing to extend herself, open her home, to care for others.

In a word: it wasn't all about Lydia.

Lydia's enduring witness through the ages isn't just about

dollars and cents. Rather, we remember Lydia—who most likely couldn't squeeze out a lot of time to browse the ancient equivalent of Target—as a woman who worked diligently with her hands and was a blessing to others.

THIRTY-FIVE DOLLARS A WEEK

I only knew Tracey for one year, when we worked together after college. Our desks faced each other, and I couldn't help but overhear the phone conversations she'd have with her husband and children. (Most phones had cords that anchored them to a wall back then.) Tracey and her husband, Daniel, had three children by birth and were fostering a sibling set of three more. The ages of this unwieldy brood ranged from two to sixteen. As you can imagine, it took a lot of communication between parents to manage that bunch.

One day after she hung up with Daniel, we chatted about grocery shopping, and Tracey told me that she fed her family on thirty-five dollars a week. I was dumbfounded. I was careful with money, but I wasn't sure I could stretch thirty-five dollars to feed *two* people! Though I don't think there was room in the tight budget for many fresh fruits and vegetables, Tracey actually fed her family on just pennies per meal.

A lot of people would look at Tracey and identify her as someone who was broke. And technically I suppose she was. But, unlike Broke Betsy, Tracey lived within her wildly limited means. She could have dug herself into debt, as Betsy had, but she chose not to. I had, and still have all these years later, such respect for a woman who used what she had to care for her family.

Guys, look for a woman like Tracey who is wise and responsible.

ANOTHER FAITHFUL STEWARD

If the New Testament Lydia, the dealer in purple cloth, were alive today, I feel certain she'd look a lot like my friend Diana Hagee. Diana, whose husband is founder of Cornerstone Church and John Hagee Ministries, is a smart, smart woman. The polar opposite of Broke Betsy, Diana is very detailed and great with money. Remember how much of Solomon's description of the Good Wife described a woman who's money savvy? That's Diana, in every way. She pays attention to the way her husband's ministry is using money, and she's not at all wasteful. Although she's a generous giver, she won't squander money carelessly. And although she could be very showy if she chose to, she's not at all flamboyant. Diana, who's wise on so many levels, is a faithful financial steward.

STOP, PAUSE, OR GO?

Pay attention to the finances of the woman you hope to marry. She doesn't need to have a big bank account, but she does need to live responsibly within her means. Keep your eyes open for the following signs.

RED FLAG

- She has more debt than she should.
- She regularly spends more than she has.
- She doesn't use everything that she's purchased.

YELLOW FLAG

- Spending gives her a rush.
- The difference between wants and needs is not clear to her.
- She assures you she'll change her spending habits after you marry.

GREEN FLAG

- She's not in debt.
- She's on top of her finances.
- She's able to give to others.

Who can find a virtuous wife?
For her worth is far above rubies.

—

Proverbs 31:10

9

MIND YOUR MANNERS WITH MARRIED MINDY

On soap operas, an affair with a married woman is often sketched out as something sultry and scandalous. Everyone knows that it's out of bounds, but that never seems to stop the devious couple from fooling around. If Warner Bros. ever featured an illicit affair between animated animals who were legally wed to other cartoon animals, there's no question that the married-woman fox fooling around with the single-man puppy would be wearing pointy ears and sporting a devil's tail. Maybe she'd be holding a pitchfork.

All this to say, in fiction, we might more easily recognize the deception and evil folly of adulterous affairs. Unfortunately, in real life, lovers—though I'd really like to challenge the working definition of *love* in this case—can much more easily fool themselves about the nature of an affair.

When Mindy sidled up to a friend of one of my sons, she wasn't wearing devil's ears or wielding a pitchfork. No, the beginnings of Mindy's relationship with a man I'll call Kevin were much more innocent.

Kevin was a youth pastor who worked with Mindy's teenage children. Mindy would visit Kevin in his office in the church basement during the week under the premise of gleaning parenting advice. (From a single twenty-eight-year-old guy who wasn't a parent. Go figure.) In the beginning the conversations revolved around Mindy's kids. But Kevin and Mindy enjoyed each other's company, and they eventually veered off to other topics.

One of those topics—which should have been taboo—was the subject of Mindy's marriage. Her husband traveled too much, she complained. When he was home he wasn't *really* home; he was preoccupied with work projects or scrolling through Facebook. He didn't take her out on dates. The picture Mindy drew for Kevin was of a marriage that was really over.

Kevin seemed completely oblivious to what was unfolding in the confines of his office. And if I were to give Mindy the benefit of the doubt, I'd concede that perhaps nothing about the poor choices she was making was malicious. (Like

I said, she wasn't wearing devil's ears.) She was lonely, and she'd found someone who made her feel less lonely. When their friendship began, Kevin innocently convinced himself that "listening" was part of his pastoral duty. Yet each week the intimacy between Kevin and Mindy grew stronger.

One afternoon Mindy rushed into Kevin's office in tears and spilled her heart out to him. She'd found e-mails, she explained, between her husband and another woman. She hadn't spoken to him about it. She hadn't turned to a sister or girlfriend. Mindy had run straight to Kevin.

It was almost as if the e-mails were the "permission" Mindy and Kevin needed to be together. They even convinced each other that maybe God had actually *given* them to each other. Mindy's marriage was over. Kevin loved her kids. Maybe God, they reasoned, was the author of this relationship that seemed *destined* to be.

That's how it started. And within a few months, Kevin and Mindy were secretly dating. Unable to see clearly, they both convinced themselves that the secrecy was an act of care for Mindy's children. It would be better for them, they assured each other. (That they didn't tell anyone else about their relationship might have also been a meaningful red flag.) Mindy never did speak to her husband about the suspicious e-mails she found. She simply allowed him to drift further away. And maybe even encouraged it.

By the time my son found out about his friend's secret

relationship, Kevin was considering proposing marriage. To a married woman! This is just a tiny taste of how deluded they were. Both Kevin and Mindy were absolutely blinded by their sin.

STEER CLEAR

Guys, unlike Trophy Tina or Prideful Peggy—where there might be a little more gray area—what I want to say to you about Mindy is pretty black and white. I don't mean simply that I find courting a married woman to be a morally evident black-and-white issue. (Which, for the record, I do.) I also suspect that you will think about Married Mindy in one of two ways.

You might think about Mindy the way I do: dating—or flirting—with a person who is married is always off-limits. No gray areas, just a red stop sign.

But perhaps you disagree. Maybe you think there might be some grayish areas that would allow you to move forward, albeit cautiously. If so, I'm going to take a guess that you already have a horse in the race. Perhaps, like Kevin, you've convinced yourself that—unlike all the other star-crossed lovers whose affairs have caused havoc for themselves and the people who love them—you're *different*. Your love is different. Your relationship is different. You will be the ones to beat the odds.

I respectfully disagree.

You cannot argue with the facts. If you're already in a relationship with a married woman, the fact is, she cheated on her husband, and there's no good reason she won't cheat on you.

Oh, you'll come up with reasons for why your choices are sound. Many of them may revolve around her first (second? third?) husband being a scumbag. And he very well may be. Some of the reasons may be about you: You're different. You love her. You're a Christian. (Let's not get into that one!) Some may even be about her: she's convinced you that you are the *one*.

Guys, if a married woman starts sending you signals, run—do not walk—to the nearest exit. Many of these relationships begin very innocently. Perhaps you notice Mindy, dissatisfied with her husband's attention, at a party. She loves having all eyes on her and may find a variety of ways to garner that attention: provocative dress, loud speech, manic karaoke. Once Mindy has your attention, she'll make you feel very special, flattering you and making you feel as though you are the center of her world.

As 1980s teens were taught to respond to drugs: Just Say No.

WE SHOULDN'T HAVE TO HAVE THIS CONVERSATION

Seriously, men, we should not even have to have this conversation. I shouldn't need to tell you not to get involved with a woman who's married. And I'd guess that, on your good days, you know this.

But where the rubber meets the road is when it's not one of your best days. Maybe you've just been dumped. Maybe you're lonely. Maybe, if you're insecure, you're very flattered by the attention of a married woman. Maybe even if you are secure, you're *still* very flattered by the attention of a married woman.

If today you decide you do not want to walk down the aisle with a woman who was married when you met her, please know that doesn't happen by accident. As will be the case with any woman you marry, the road to the wedding aisle is paved with lots of choices that are seemingly much smaller than the moment you pull a Tiffany box out of your jacket pocket to propose.

You need to decide today that you will not have any overly intimate conversations with a woman who's married. If she tries to tell you that her husband is a cad, that she's wildly unhappy, that their marriage has been over for years, simply suggest that you are not the person with whom she needs to share this information. This is the stuff for pastors, for counselors, for sisters, for mothers. It is not for you. You don't need to exchange playful, knowing glances. You don't need to be alone in rooms together. If this woman's marriage truly *is* struggling, I can be very certain when I tell you: you are not the person God has chosen to help her.

If you hear that lying voice in your ear telling you that you should listen, or that you should love—know you are hearing the voice of the deceiver! That is not God's voice.

Precious young men, in many ways Married Mindy can be the easiest woman to avoid becoming entangled with. Though few things in this world are black and white, this one actually is. A woman who is married is *not* the woman for you.

A WIFE OF NOBLE CHARACTER

In his wise exhortations about the type of woman to marry, Solomon asked, "Who can find a virtuous wife?" In the same breath he added, "For her worth is far above rubies" (Proverbs 31:10).

If you think about it, it's really sort of an odd juxtaposition.

On one hand, to search for a woman of good character seems like a no-brainer for any guy on a wife hunt. Am I right? Of course you want a woman of integrity and character. Solomon shouldn't have to waste his breath, or the ink of his pen, to remind us that this is the woman who makes a Good Wife. I don't know the ancient Hebrew word for *obviously*, but . . . *obviously*.

So when Solomon says that a godly woman is worth more than rubies, it makes me stop and think. If this is just a given, a morally obvious requirement for one's lifelong partner, why does he value good character above even precious gems? My guess is that it's because a woman without good character will corrode an entire marriage.

Choosing a wife with dark hair or light hair will be your choice. Whether she's short or tall, light skinned or dark skinned, English speaking or Spanish speaking are all matters of personal preference. What's nonnegotiable, however, is *character*.

As you consider the woman you will marry, it should be plainly evident that you don't choose someone who is currently married. That should be (although it doesn't always seem to be) a Marriage 101 no-brainer.

I want to push you a bit further, though, to pursue a woman whose character could be called noble. That's taking it to the next level, isn't it? The woman of noble character not only is not going to date someone else when she's married— yikes!—but she's not going to flirt with your colleagues at the office Christmas party. You're not going to need to "accidentally" check her text messages to know what she's up to. When you've found a woman of noble character, you've found a woman you can *trust*.

ABOVE AND BEYOND THE CALL OF DUTY

A woman in the Bible who's been widely recognized across centuries and cultures as a woman of noble character is one who demonstrated faithfulness, integrity, and sacrifice in relationship with her husband's mother. The contrast between Married Mindy and Ruth is stark: Mindy, who seeks her own happiness, cannot remain faithful to a husband who is living; Ruth was so faithful to her husband and his family that—at great sacrifice—she committed herself to remain faithful and seek the good of her deceased husband's mother, Naomi.

The backstory is that although Naomi was an Israelite, during a famine her family had gone to live in the country of Moab, to the south of Israel. Like a Canadian couple who'd moved to Mexico City for business, raised their sons there, and watched them marry Mexican women, Naomi's sons naturally grew up and married women from Moab. And yet when Naomi's story opens in the book of Ruth, we discover that Naomi's husband and two sons have died. Without the protection of their menfolk, Naomi and her daughters-in-law were very vulnerable in Moab. They needed to find security.

The wife of one of Naomi's sons, Orpah, did exactly what one would expect. She returned to her family. There was nothing shameful about this; it was what anyone would expect of a widowed daughter-in-law.

Just as no one would expect a widowed young Mexican woman to leave her family and her roots in order to venture off to Canada with her widowed mother-in-law, it was equally absurd that Ruth would commit her life and her future to a grieving mother-in-law from a completely foreign country. But that's exactly what happened. Ruth's radical fidelity—when, unlike Married Mindy's selfish actions, pursuing her own happiness would have been completely acceptable—is captured in the words she spoke to Naomi:

> But Ruth said, "Entreat me not to leave you, / Or to turn back from following after you; / For wherever you go, I will go; / And wherever you lodge, I will lodge; / Your people shall be my people, / And your God, my God. / Where you die, I will die, / And there will I be buried. / The LORD do so to me, and more also, / If anything but death parts you and me." (Ruth 1:16–17)

Many who aren't familiar with the Bible, who've heard this passage at weddings, are surprised to discover that these words weren't spoken to a spouse. They were spoken by Ruth to a mother-in-law who was returning to a foreign land with a foreign tongue and a foreign culture. Sacrificing her own happiness for the sake of her mother-in-law's—not to mention the possibility of rekindling an old flame with the guy who'd taken her to prom—is radically divergent from the type of self-serving woman we see in Mindy.

As it turned out, Ruth did catch the eye of one of Naomi's relatives in Israel, and they married and had children. And as it unfolded even further, Ruth became the great-great-grand-mother to Solomon, who would eventually write, "Who can find a virtuous wife? / For her worth is far above rubies" (Proverbs 31:10).

He knew what he was talking about.

A MOTHER-IN-LAW'S DREAM

Guys, not only do you want to avoid dating and marrying a woman who's married, but you also want to avoid marrying one who will *become* Married Mindy by cheating on you. That my son married a woman who will never become a Married Mindy is one of my greatest joys. Meredith is an ab-solute delight. Every mama's dream, she is full of knowledge of the Scriptures. Not just head knowledge either—Meredith has a heart for the Lord. If there was ever an anti-Mindy, Meredith would be her! I'm fully confident that her heart, mind, and body are committed to Kyle.

One of the things I noticed about Meredith when she and Kyle were dating was the way she spoke about her dad. She was nuts about him. This isn't to say she wasn't aware of his shortcomings; she was. She saw him realistically and had a heart full of grace toward him. When I noticed that, I thought, *This girl will also be gracious toward my son.* Years later, I'm delighted to report it is true.

Pam Thum Marshall is another amazing married woman who is a close friend of mine. Pam is a well-known worship leader and songwriter. She is not only a beautiful person outwardly but she is also a beautiful woman inwardly. She is an asset to her husband, Stephen. Pam had a successful singing career prior to her marrying Stephen. She did not allow that to keep her from merging her career with his. Today they both have a very successful career--not separate but together as one.

Gentlemen, as you seek to avoid Married Mindy, don't assume that if you've found a woman who's single, you're home free. I encourage you to go even further and pursue a woman who'll *remain* faithful to you. Search for a godly woman who will honor you as you honor her.

STOP, PAUSE, OR GO?

You know not to become involved with a woman who's married. Obviously. But I want you to be cognizant of other signs that might reveal her future fidelity to you as well.

RED FLAG

- She's married.
- She flirts with married men.
- She has a history of cheating.

YELLOW FLAG

- She complains to you about her husband.
- She's seriously dating or engaged to someone else.
- She doesn't have a problem with other people cheating.

GREEN FLAG

- She's single.
- She maintains healthy boundaries with married men.
- She's considered by others to be a woman of noble character.

She opens her mouth with wisdom,
And on her tongue is the law of kindness.

—

Proverbs 31:26

10

LEAVE BEHIND LYING LINDA

Linda lived several doors down from our new home. I'd been stretching out front after a nice walk when she invited me over for coffee. Though I had a to-do list that didn't quit, I took a quick shower and headed over to her home for a visit.

As Linda escorted me through her foyer, I noticed a gorgeous painting in her living room. The scene of a turbulent ocean at sunset was one of the most dynamic oil paintings I'd ever seen.

"Linda, I love that painting," I cooed. "It has so much energy."

"Meryl Streep used to own it," she explained. "I found it in a funky little vintage consignment shop when we lived in LA. It cost an arm and a leg, but we like it."

"Hmm," I mused. I wondered momentarily what Meryl Streep's painting had been doing in a consignment shop. Surely that girl wasn't pawning treasures to pay her bills.

Linda led me into the kitchen and invited me to sit down in a sunny little breakfast nook. She'd put out a basket of muffins she must have made during my shower. As we were getting settled, we heard her phone ringing. It sounded a bit muffled.

"Excuse me," she said. "Let me find that!"

She began digging through her handbag. The phone rang a few more times. When she finally found it, she peeked at it and explained apologetically, "Mary, I'm so sorry. I need to grab this."

"Of course," I assured her. "No problem."

As she stepped into the next room, Linda answered her phone, "This is Linda . . . I'm sorry I couldn't get to the phone. It was in the back of my closet."

Back of her closet? What an odd thing to say, I thought.

I glanced around Linda's kitchen, noticing the photos on her fridge. A few showed two teenage girls I assumed to be her daughters dressed in soccer uniforms. As Linda continued talking on the phone, I heard her arguing with someone.

"Well, I'm a licensed real estate attorney, so I think I know."

As the conversation became more heated, I felt a bit uncomfortable hearing the whole exchange.

When Linda hung up, she swooped back into the kitchen.

"I'm so sorry about that. The Merkands next door have installed a bright light on their back patio that shines all night long. My girls sleep on the north side of the house," Linda explained, thumbing her hand in the direction of the Merkands' home. "They say it doesn't bother them, but I think it's entirely unacceptable."

So that's how I discovered that the picturesque neighborhood we'd chosen to live in was like anyplace else where there are, well, people.

"Did I hear you say you're a real estate attorney?" I asked, eager to move on from the awkward phone call and learn more about Linda.

"I was a paralegal for five years," she offered. Her tone communicated that she found that to be a perfectly reasonable explanation for claiming to be an attorney. "So I know we have rights."

Linda's phone rang again. She peeked at the caller ID and explained, "I'm going to grab this and then turn this phone *off*."

"That's fine," I said, though I did hope it was the last interruption.

Linda sat down opposite me as she picked up the call. Glancing out the window, I noticed a delivery truck in front of the house.

"No, I'm not home right now," Linda fibbed. "I should

be back . . . umm . . . in about two hours. But we leave for vacation in the morning, so I do need it this afternoon. Thank you."

She switched off her phone and set it on the counter. "That was the delivery guy for something I ordered. They can deliver it later so that we can visit now."

Suddenly I was Linda's top priority.

"But I think they're right out front," I said, pointing out the front window toward the truck.

"They'll be back," she assured me. "They don't mind."

If I were the delivery guy and saw us sipping java in the kitchen, I think I'd mind. Still, eager to get to know Linda, I queried, "So where are you going tomorrow?"

"What do you mean?" she asked, genuinely stumped.

"I mean, where are you going on vacation? Flying someplace, or driving?"

"Oh!" She nodded, suddenly understanding what I meant. "Oh, no, we're not going anywhere. I just didn't want him to think I was going to go pick up that package at the warehouse."

She said it as if the driver were the one trying to pull a fast one on *her*.

After she shut off her phone, Linda and I actually had a lovely visit. But I couldn't shake the lingering question of whether anything she told me was true.

Did Meryl Streep ever own that painting?

TROUBLE SEPARATING TRUTH FROM FICTION

Lying Linda has chronic difficulty telling the truth. It's not that she stretches the truth a wee bit. In fact, it's unclear whether Linda even recognizes what is truth and what is fiction.

Linda's lying is corrosive to her relationships. I know I would be very cautious about developing a deeper friendship with her. And if it only took me a few moments to catch on to Linda's "innocent" deceptions, I couldn't imagine what it would be like to be her husband or her daughters.

Linda's lies serve one person: Linda. Without even seeming to realize what she's up to, she offers an explanation that will impress or threaten. She misleads to suggest she's a little more than she actually is. She twists the truth for her own convenience. And because she's fed this monster of deception for so long, sometimes she'll lie for no reason at all. ("Back of my closet"? Really? Why?)

Some of Linda's lies just stretch the truth, and some are whoppers. Over the course of our conversation that day, I found myself wondering: Had her daughter *really* been offered a full-ride soccer scholarship to Duke? Did her husband *really* invent the cell phone charger? Could she *really* have been neighbors with Kobe Bryant, Sally Field, Tom Cruise, *and* Miley Cyrus?

Pieces of a Lying Linda's stories will be true, but there's no reliable way to know which parts. (Maybe she just saw

Miley Cyrus on TV at the Grammys and it *felt* like they were neighbors.) And anyone who tries to question her lies will see the claws come out. When Linda feels backed into a corner—by pesky "truth"—she is prone to attack. Because she doesn't want to be exposed as a fraud, she'll lash out and, quite creatively, make the conflict about you. *Your* misgivings. *Your* suspicions. *Your* accusations. By the end of your conversation you might actually believe you are in the wrong for even questioning Linda's version of reality.

READ THE SIGNS

Guys, open your eyes.

During the courtship period, Linda's deceptions could be easy to miss. Until you know each other well, you might not recognize some of the tall tales she's spinning. As always, pay attention to the way the woman you are with relates to others. For example, let's say you're with her and is running late to visit her parents. When they call to see where she is, how does she respond?

- "Mom, this is crazy. We got a flat, but we're back on the road now. We'll be there in twenty."
- "We ran out of gas! It was his car, so at least it wasn't my fault. My sweetie had a gas can in his trunk so we just walked to a gas station and filled it up."

- "Mom, I didn't plan well. It was a busy day, and I just didn't leave enough time to get ready. So sorry. We'll see you in twenty."

The first explanation conveniently relieves her of all responsibility for her tardiness. The second, as I suspect you noticed, implicates *you* in the debacle. In the third, though, she tells the truth when it's the more difficult of the two options. Given a choice between an easy option and a difficult one, Linda will choose what is easiest for her.

What I want you to hear and understand is that you will not escape being affected by this web of lies. Maybe you'll start to notice the way Linda stretches the truth to enhance a story she's telling. It seems harmless at first. Then perhaps you'll start to pick up on some of Linda's other fibs. You'll begin to realize that Linda lies without even intending to. You'll notice that, because the filter through which she sees the world is to behave in ways that benefit her, she can no longer distinguish between what is true and what is false.

In time you'll realize that you cannot trust Linda about *anything*. Her lies have eroded trust between you, and when that happens your love will dry up. You'll look at her and see a shell of a person you once thought you knew. It's not possible to be intimate with someone as slippery as Linda.

THE TRUSTWORTHY WIFE

Solomon reflected on this woman of integrity in his description of the Good Wife. He declared that she was a woman who could be trusted: "She opens her mouth with wisdom, / And on her tongue is the law of kindness" (Proverbs 31:26).

You might imagine her as a vessel. On the inside, her deep places are full of truth, wisdom, and integrity. When she speaks, this is what naturally comes forth from her mouth. Sometimes her wisdom and faithful instruction are well received, and other times they may not be. But the woman Solomon described, the one you know that you can trust, is brave to speak truth in every situation.

Lying Linda, however, is filled with lies, foolishness, and moral flimsiness. Her insides are poisoned with deception. When Linda speaks, this is what flows from her tongue.

Jesus saved His most harsh criticism for those who behave the way Linda behaves. Centuries after Solomon identified the good and faithful wife, Jesus also described what is true of human beings: our lips reveal what is inside of us, and what is inside of us cannot help but spill off our lips. And although there's a popular cultural stereotype about Jesus being a groovy, peaceful hippie who's tirelessly "nice," He reserved His harshest criticism for the religious leaders who had no more integrity than Lying Linda.

"Either make the tree good and its fruit good, or else make the tree bad and its fruit bad; for a tree is known by its

LEAVE BEHIND LYING LINDA

fruit" (Matthew 12:33). What's internal, He was saying, is evident by what you produce externally.

He continued to lay in to those false teachers:

> Brood of vipers! How can you, being evil, speak good things? For out of the abundance of the heart the mouth speaks. A good man out of the good treasure of his heart brings forth good things, and an evil man out of the evil treasure brings forth evil things. But I say to you that for every idle word men may speak, they will give account of it in the day of judgment. For by your words you will be justified, and by your words you will be condemned. (Matthew 12:34–37)

Jesus wanted us to know that what we speak matters. It matters because it impacts our relationship with God and our relationships with others. Lying Linda is unable to speak with wisdom or offer faithful instruction because what's inside of her has been revealed—by her own speech—to be corroded.

BRAVELY DARING TO TELL THE TRUTH

In the beginning, Lying Linda tells a lie when it is easier than telling the truth. She chooses the way that makes her look good, the easy way. Eventually, losing all track of reality, she lies when there is no reason to lie. Her insides have been corrupted by deceit and she can no longer distinguish truth.

The woman to marry, I'll suggest, is a woman who does exactly the opposite. When this woman is in the most difficult of circumstances, when she's afraid that telling the truth will have negative consequences in her life, she bravely speaks the truth anyway.

One of the biblical women we see doing this is a most unlikely lady. In fact, had she not encountered Jesus, she would have, according to the social hierarchy of her culture, been entirely overlooked.

Warning: guys, I'm about to talk "lady business," but I want you to trust me enough to hang in here with me!

Capernaum was on the northern shore of the Sea of Galilee. Not very dense at all, there might have been just a few rows of houses along the shore. It was located, though, on a major highway. No, there weren't cars or trucks, but it was a busy thoroughfare.

According to Mark 5, one day Jesus was heading to the house of a local synagogue leader but was pressed by eager crowds. One of the people in the crush was a woman who'd been bleeding for twelve years. Besides the brutal toll this would have taken on her body, the impact would have rippled through every other area of her life as well. Socially, women were expected to stay indoors during their monthly flow, so she was breaking the law by even being in public. Too, seeking help from all kinds of doctors and healers would have left her, and her family, financially bankrupt.

But when this woman heard about a miracle man, she dared to hope once more. Battling her way through the crowd, the woman reached out to touch the edge of Jesus' clothing. When she did, she knew—in her deep places—that she'd been healed.

And here's where it gets real: the woman was immediately terrified, because not only had she violated the purity laws, but now she'd gone even further to touch a rabbi, making Him unclean. This meant that both of them would have had to endure a process of ritual cleansing.

"Who touched Me?" Jesus asked.

His disciples must have thought He was nuts! A better question in that crowd might have been, "Who didn't touch Me?"

In that moment, when no one really could have discerned *who* touched Jesus, the easiest thing to do would have been to lie. The most difficult thing? For the woman to come forward and confess what she had done. But that's exactly what this unnamed lady did, fully expecting to be shamed and scorned.

She wasn't, though. Instead, Jesus kindly called her "daughter" and blessed her (Mark 5:34).

Guys, the kind of woman you want to marry is one who not only tells the truth when it's convenient, it's a woman who—like the one who'd been bleeding for twelve years— tells the truth when it's most difficult.

COURAGEOUS TRANSPARENCY

Lying Linda tells half-truths and untruths to make herself look better to others than she actually is. But I knew a girl in college who was the diametric opposite of Lying Linda. What I recall about Raylene, what strikes me as so unique, is that she was willing for others to see who she *really* was. This is just a small thing, but if Raylene got up late and had to choose between looking fantastic and making it to class, she'd go to class—still looking presentable, but without makeup.

I also remember she was quick to take responsibility when something was her fault. It's funny I even remember this, but when one of our dorm showers got backed up, I remember Linda—who had long, thick dark hair—digging around the drain to clean out the hair.

Or when others in our hallway were complaining one night about getting Bs or Cs—as if it had been the teacher's fault!—I remember Raylene confessing that she'd gotten a C in chemistry because she just didn't turn in some of the assignments.

What I found most compelling about Raylene was her transparency. She was such a breath of fresh air because she didn't spend a lot of energy trying to convince others she was better than she actually was. This kind of transparency is the opposite of Lying Linda, who's more concerned with how she's seen than with what is true.

Guys, look for a woman who's secure enough about who she is that she doesn't need to hide and cover up like Lying Linda.

THE KIND OF TRUTH THAT SETS PEOPLE FREE

If Lying Linda is always using a measure of deceit to put herself in the best possible light, one remarkable woman I know has done *exactly* the opposite.

Lisa Bevere is one of the most transparent people I know. For more than two decades, Lisa and her husband, John, have served together through Messenger International, an organization committed to teach, reach, and rescue by communicating God's Word and love in action around the world. Lisa connects with women on a heart level as she humbly shares her own personal struggles and experiences to empower lives with freedom and transformation.

Her honesty hasn't hindered her husband. It has actually opened doors for both of them. This kind of transparency is the opposite of Lying Linda, who's more concerned with how she's seen than with what is true.

STOP, PAUSE, OR GO?

The Good Wife will be a woman who not only avoids bold-faced lies but is also passionate about clinging to the truth. Keep your antennae up to discern whether she's a woman of integrity.

RED FLAG

- She lies.
- She distorts the truth.
- She says whatever is most convenient in the moment.

YELLOW FLAG

- She "embellishes" stories a bit too much.
- She accuses *you* of lying. (When you haven't!)
- She says whatever she believes will make her look good.

GREEN FLAG

- She tells the truth.
- She tells the truth when it's hard.
- Others trust her.

She seeks wool and flax,
And willingly works with her hands.

—

Proverbs 31:13

11

LET GO OF LAZY LUCY

My friend Lucy, from the office where I worked, had kindly offered to lend me an exercise ball she was no longer using. She'd suggested she could bring it to me at work, but as I was doing errands one evening, I ended up in the heart of her neighborhood and decided just to stop in to save her the trouble.

When Lucy peeked through the peephole and carefully unlatched her door, she appeared surprised, and possibly a bit concerned, that I'd dropped by unannounced. She cracked the door only about eighteen inches as we chatted. Sensing the evident tension, I apologized for surprising her and explained the reason for my visit.

As Lucy opened the door for me to step inside, I couldn't

believe what I was seeing. Her home was piled high with stacks of papers, magazines, and assorted odds and ends. She couldn't invite me to sit down because every seat—including the couch, chairs, and kitchen stools—were covered! Amid the papers and knickknacks were what appeared to be several days' worth of empty glasses and dirty plates. When Lucy had told me that she often spent four to five hours each evening watching television, I hadn't believed her. Now I did.

I stood frozen in the entryway. I remembered she'd once or twice joked about how she too often chose to veg out on the couch and catch up on her TiVo shows rather than clean her house, but I had thought she was kidding. I realized now she hadn't been. In fact, it looked like the place hadn't been cleaned for weeks.

Lucy, anxious, instructed, "Stay here. I'll go get it."

As she turned to go for the exercise ball, she brushed against a stack of mail, which tumbled to the ground.

"I can get that," I offered, bending down.

"No, no," she said. "I'll sort that later. You just sit tight."

When Lucy disappeared down the hallway, I looked around. Dust lined the windowsills and tables. Dingy drapes covered the windows. Plates and bowls with dried food littered the counters.

I have to say, I was really surprised. Lucy usually looked mostly put together when I saw her at work. Yes, there was sometimes a stain on her shirt or cat hair on her slacks. And, yes, a peek into her car in the office lot sometimes revealed a Burger King wrapper, banana peel, or empty Diet Coke can or two. But I hadn't imagined that she would let her place get to this level of dirtiness. The mess Lucy lived in wouldn't qualify her for an episode of *Hoarders*—it wasn't that bad—but it was disconcerting.

When Lucy returned with the ball, I thanked her and quickly turned to leave.

"Thanks for stopping by, Mary," Lucy said. "And I'm sorry I didn't have a chance to straighten up for you."

I smiled politely, but inside I was calculating that I would've had to have given her a couple of days' notice to provide ample "straightening" time.

When I got home, I shared the perplexing scene with Don and decided not to mention it to anyone else. But when our mutual friend Sarah, from the office, heard about the loan of the exercise ball, she broached the subject with me in the office break room.

"So," asked Sarah, "did you pick up the exercise ball at Lucy's apartment?"

Not wanting to open the door for gossip, I answered with only two words: "I did." I purposed to sound neither horrified nor disgusted. And, if I do say so myself, I think I pulled off a pretty impressive picture of *nonchalant*.

That was all Sarah needed, though, to dish on Lucy's

housekeeping habits. I didn't like where the conversation was headed, but then Sarah suddenly surprised me.

"Mary," she explained with a kindness and compassion I'd not expected, "what you were seeing was the inside of her heart."

Sarah's words landed in my own heart, and I continued to think on them throughout the week. My gut told me she'd hit on something true, and I wanted to know what it was. But as I was not a trained interpreter, I couldn't tell you exactly what that chaotic glimpse into Lucy's heart revealed.

The concern of my heart was that it revealed something about how Lucy saw herself.

CHAOTIC HEART

My concerns about Lucy lingered. It wasn't just that she didn't keep a Martha Stewart perfect home either. Lucy's condition, I feared, wasn't something a housecleaner hired to do a deep clean could fix. The way her physical environment had spiraled out of control signaled something much deeper.

Jesus said that the two most important commandments are to love God and love our neighbors as we love ourselves (Mark 12:28–29). What we sometimes don't hear and appreciate, however, is that Jesus assumed that we love ourselves. Our love for others is predicated on this assumption that we do love ourselves and that if we love others in equal measure, everyone wins.

Sadly, it's not evident that Lazy Lucy does exercise care for herself. That means that if she loves *you* the way she loves herself—sloppy clothing, unwashed dishes, a chaotic environment—you won't be *loved* well. In fact, when a Lucy marries young, she becomes a woman who does not know how to remove a gas cap to fill up her car with gas, doesn't know how to use the ATM, and can't find a job on her own. And while you might feel heroic at first, doing these things for Lucy, the novelty will quickly wear off.

The condition of Lucy's home *now* will be the condition of *your* home in the future. If you're looking for a clean spoon or dish, you'll be doing a lot of dishwashing. Clean laundry? Only if you get lucky and find it in the dryer with a load you started last night. If you marry Lazy Lucy, you're in for a heap of frustration in the years to come. The woman who can't love herself will not be able to love you.

When I stopped by the home of my Lucy, it wasn't clear to me if she realized she was in a problematic situation. She seemed a bit uncomfortable with my arrival, which told me she knew *something* was wrong. And yet she'd apparently been living in those conditions for so long she lacked what was required to *respond* to that knowing. Similar, I suppose, to those who do live with clinical hoarding diagnoses, Lucy seemed immobilized, unable to change the circumstances that I believe she did recognize as being less than optimal.

LOOSING LUCY

As I've thought about Lucy over the years, I've wondered how I'd react if one of my sons or grandsons brought her home to meet Don and me. Perhaps it would be a young woman who could pass muster at work or at church but whose private life was wildly disordered. And if I'm honest, I would need to suggest to my beloved boys that they *pass* on her.

I'm not saying Lucy is worthless. She's not. She's made in the image of God the same way you and I are. I encourage you to be her friend, but I wouldn't counsel you to marry Lucy. She's simply not in the kind of emotionally and spiritually healthy place that a *wife* needs to be in, in order to give and receive in a mutually beneficial relationship.

Men, I'm going to shoot straight with you: Lucy is a woman who needs to be taken care of. If you marry her, you will be doing just that for the rest of your life. She won't be the mutual helpmate you need to create a marriage in which both people flourish.

Every person needs to know how to take care of themselves and their homes. Whether you'll do this in your own home or whether you'll one day hire someone to care for things, you need to have the will and the skill to care for yourself. So does your wife. Sadly, Lazy Lucy is unable to care for herself, and she will be unable to care for you or for your kids.

WORKING WITH EAGER HANDS

Remember Broke Betsy? Whether Betsy makes a great salary or whether she brings home pennies, she is *stuck* because she's always spending more than she has. What a woman does with her money is one area King Solomon addressed in Proverb 31. The Good Wife is the one who is responsible and savvy with what she's been given.

The other major thing Solomon had to say about a woman's work is related to industry. Productivity. Commitment to the work she's chosen. Solomon said of the Good Wife, "She seeks wool and flax, / And willingly works with her hands" (Proverbs 31:13). The Good Wife is not the one who's *forced* to contribute to the family's finances and well-being—through work outside the home or work within the home—she's the one who is *eager* to be productive by doing meaningful work.

Peek again at Solomon's description in Proverbs 31 of the work that the Good Wife does. While some of these qualities expose the folly of Betsy's irresponsibility as an out-of-control spender, many also expose the laziness of Lucy. The woman who's exalted as the blessed wife who is to be praised is the one who applies her heart, soul, mind, and strength to the tasks before her:

- "She seeks wool and flax, / And willingly works with her hands" (v. 13). Her hands are raring to go!

- "She also rises while it is yet night, / And provides food for her household, / And a portion for her maidservants" (v. 15). She rises before the sun!
- "She considers a field and buys it; / From her profits she plants a vineyard" (v. 16). She's a farming machine!
- "She girds herself with strength, / And strengthens her arms" (v. 17). She's strong and energetic!
- "She perceives that her merchandise is good, / And her lamp does not go out by night" (v. 18). She stays up later than the sun!
- "She watches over the ways of her household, / And does not eat the bread of idleness" (v. 27). She's not lazy!

Of all the women I'm warning you to be cautious about, Lazy Lucy is as much the polar opposite of the composite sketch of the Proverbs 31 woman as any of the others to be avoided.

THE ANCIENT MARTHA STEWART

Centuries after Solomon described our hardworking Good Wife, in first-century Israel we catch a glimpse of just such a woman. Though she didn't seem to have a husband, Martha is a model countertype to Lazy Lucy.

Though I realize it's a coincidence that the biblical

Martha bears the same name as the modern domestic diva Martha Stewart, the likeness need not be overlooked. Both of these Marthas are industrious, diligent, hardworking, and hospitable. If any first-century woman might have had an empire built on domestic duty and hospitality, it would have been Mary and Lazarus's sister and Jesus' friend, Martha.

Of the glimpses we get of Martha in the Gospels, the one that's the most well known often gives Martha a bad rap. The moral we've gleaned from the encounter Jesus had in the home of His friends is too often reduced to "Don't be like Martha." I'd like to suggest that there's much more to this woman.

When Jesus visited the home of Lazarus, Mary, and Martha, where He'd often stay, many, including His disciples, had gathered to hear Jesus' teaching. They'd crowded into the home to sit at the feet of the controversial rabbi. While Mary joined the other guests, Martha was busy with the preparations that were needed to host this hungry crew.

Guys, I'm going to let you in on a secret: when we women read this story from Luke's gospel, we're torn. On the one hand, we hear the words of Jesus. And at some level we even understand. We know that—in the big picture—given the choice between sitting at the feet of Jesus and scrambling around like a housemaid, we'd prefer to kick back and spend time with the Master. But we'd also be aware that the Master was probably thirsty. He and His buddies would be getting hungry. They'd need to wash up after a dusty day on the road. I don't know a woman who wouldn't be torn between these two possibilities.

No, scratch that. The woman who would not be torn is named Lucy.

And although Luke doesn't mention it (maybe because he's a guy?), I have to believe that unless Mary was completely oblivious, she, too, was torn between the two ideals. There, in her own living room, was the One who had the Words of Life. Who'd want to be drawing water and cooking the lentils? And yet Mary did understand that—in her culture and in ours—it would have been the responsibility of the hostess to serve her guests. My gut tells me that some part of Mary was wrestling with her responsibility, even as Jesus spoke.

I'd assume that was true of Martha also. She knew and loved and trusted Jesus. Of *course* she wanted to be chilling at His feet and eating up the words He was offering! But she was also aware that there were other hungry people in her home. And as Jesus fed hearts, Martha chose to feed hungry bodies.

Listen to the words Jesus spoke to Martha when she begged Him to send Mary into the kitchen: "Martha, Martha, you are worried and troubled about many things. But one thing is needed, and Mary has chosen that good part, which will not be taken away from her" (Luke 10:41–42).

This is where Martha gets the bad rap. I've heard the passage read from the pulpit with a condemning tone. But Jesus' relationship with Martha—one in which she clearly loves and trusts Jesus—suggests to me that these words He spoke were slathered in love and affection. *The Message*, Eugene Peterson's translation of the Bible, gets at this fondness a bit: "Martha, dear Martha, you're fussing far too much and getting yourself worked up over nothing. One thing only is essential, and Mary has chosen it—it's the main course, and it won't be taken from her." Jesus isn't saying that what Martha is doing is unimportant. In some ways—by feeding hungry people—they're both doing the same thing. Jesus is asking Martha to have perspective about the situation.

As I mentioned when we met Holy Holly, you want to choose a woman who *does* feast from the table Jesus prepares. That's what Mary is doing in this story. But I also want you to hear Solomon's exhortation to choose a woman who "willingly works with her hands" (Proverbs 31:13). Martha is that eager servant who cares for the people in her home.

And after the dishes are cleared and cleaned, she settles in to be fed by the One who is the Bread of Life.

THE FIRST MRS. COLBERT

One of many things I most appreciate about my mother-in-law is that she raised three incredible children. (Thank you, Kitty, for the gift of Don.) But it's not just what she did during her children's formative years that I admire about this strong woman of God. It's who she is today. Though our modern indulgent "retirement" decades couldn't have been imagined by those in the biblical narratives, the woman I once called Mrs. Colbert (before I became Mrs. Colbert) is an active, vibrant woman without a lazy bone in her body. Not only does she serve at her church and advocate for homeless animals, but Kitty still works full-time at a local bank. Because I don't want to add to her workload, I won't mention the name of the bank. But if you were to call Anytown Bank during normal business hours, the voice you'd hear on the other end, the one that would get you the help you needed, would be Kitty Colbert's.

Kitty's vibrant, industrious life reminds me of the parable of Jesus and the fig tree. Jesus didn't curse the fig tree because He didn't like figs; Jesus cursed the fig tree when it stopped producing figs (Matthew 21:18–20). Though I'm not in the habit of giving proper names to trees, the fruitless fig tree would be named Lazy Lucy.

Gentlemen, keep your eyes open for the type of woman Don's father married, a woman like Kitty Colbert who works with energy, enthusiasm, and faithfulness.

WORKING AT THE CAR WASH

When her husband first noticed her, Joyce Meyer—now a world-renowned Bible teacher—was washing her mother's car. That no-nonsense work ethic is one that has continued throughout their marriage. Not only is Joyce professionally industrious, but she has also cared for her home and raised her kids with structure and order. Perhaps the best way to say it is that there is a spirit of *excellence* about Joyce. She has incredible stamina as well. And unlike Lazy Lucy, she's attentive to detail. Joyce embodies so many qualities of the woman Solomon described in Proverbs 31.

STOP, PAUSE, OR GO?

One of the problems with Lazy Lucy—which will become your problem—is that she doesn't do her share. Though there may be a variety of reasons for this, they may not matter. You'll do well to heed these warning signs.

RED FLAG

- She doesn't know how to care for herself or her things.
- She refuses to learn to care for herself or her things.
- Someone else has always taken care of her needs.

YELLOW FLAG

- She isn't willing to get up and go in the mornings.
- Her home is disheveled.
- Her car is a dumping ground.

GREEN FLAG

- She's eager to contribute.
- She's a hard worker.
- Her work is profitable.

She girds herself with strength,
And strengthens her arms.
—

Proverbs 31:17

12

STAY AWAY FROM SAD SALLY

"Life's hard. Then you die."

This is how an acquaintance of mine, Sally, views her life. (And it is, in my opinion, a really lovely life!) Sally is in her early forties, she's an office manager at a local pharmaceutical company, and she's married to a great guy. They have one son and one daughter who are fourth and fifth graders at the school where Eric, her husband, teaches kindergarten.

Sally is usually upset or disappointed about *something*. Depending on the given day, she might be feeling disappointed because she doesn't get to drive her kids to and from school—or feeling low when Eric has to be at school for a morning meeting or stay into the evening, because then she *has* to drive her children.

Lose-lose. This is how Sally sees her past, her present, and her future.

Because Sally does tend to pour out her woes when we get together, I wasn't surprised, when we grabbed coffee a few weeks ago, that the conversation took a turn to such matters. One of her children had been hospitalized with bronchitis, and somehow Sally sort of made that be about *her*. But what Sally shared shed some real light on her heart.

I knew that Sally's family, going back several generations on both sides, was from Minnesota. Sipping a tall Starbucks Mocha Frappuccino, Sally told me that when she was young, the only work her father could find was in California. So the whole family—parents, six-year-old Sally, and her three-year-old sister, Marian—moved to San Diego for him to take a job in a factory. Seven months after they arrived, however, Sally's little sister, Marian, contracted spinal meningitis.

While Marian was hospitalized, Sally's mom was torn between trying to be near the quarantined toddler in the hospital and being at home to care for Sally. The family didn't have any extra money to spare for a sitter, and even the public transportation to and from the hospital proved to be an expense that stretched them. So when Sally finished first grade that June, her mother sent her back to her grandparents who lived in a small farm town outside of Minneapolis. She thought that each of her girls would be better served this way. Sally, surrounded by cousins and corn and cows and chickens, would live with her grandparents while her mother managed Marian's care.

"Everything was always about my cousin Judy," Sally groaned. "She had the nicest clothes, nicest shoes. Her parents spoiled her, and she got whatever she wanted."

I could understand how Sally could have felt competition for her grandparents' attention, with so many cousins nearby, and also envious of a girl her age who was smothered with her own mother's love and attention.

"Wow," I marveled, savoring a sip of my tea, "that must have been difficult."

Sally nodded. "It was. And it hasn't ended with Judy. She married a doctor who still pampers her the way everybody did growing up. He buys her flowers, he is always buying her gifts, and he washes her car . . ."

Sally continued the litany as if she were reciting a record of crimes committed against humanity. I tried to appear sympathetic, but I was really thinking, *I don't think any of that stuff—including the preferential treatment as a child—is really Judy's fault.* I bit my lip.

"I've never had that," she moaned. "I don't have people cooking for me and cleaning for me and running errands for me."

Now the list of criminal charges was getting longer. I knew Sally's husband well, and I'd spent time with them as a couple and in the context of our families being together. He might not get her flowers every week, but John was really a kind and generous guy.

I wanted to tell Sally that in this world very few people have others waiting on them hand and foot, but I doubted it would make a difference.

What was really helpful for me in this conversation was knowing what Sally's sixth year of life had been like. During that year she hadn't felt like she got what she needed: love, attention, clothing. And it was as if that experience had sort of solidified, hardening Sally's heart from receiving and recognizing the blessings in her life. From my vantage point, I could see many ways Sally was getting what she needed, but through the lens by which Sally saw the world, she only recognized the *absence* and want. Though she attended church, it wasn't clear that she'd encountered and come to trust a generous Provider. Sally had it in her head that things would never go her way, that she'd never get what she needed.

And, in Sally's mind, she never did.

EVERY GLASS HALF EMPTY

When you consider Sad Sally, it's important to know that this is not someone who battles clinical depression. My husband, Don, encounters many such women in his practice—individuals whose neurotransmitters are out of whack. Clinical depression is more than a temporary feeling of sadness. It's different from feeling occasionally down. It's not the same thing as being in a bad mood.

It's also not Sad Sally.

Sad Sally is the kind of gal who sees the half-full glass as being half empty. If something is going to go wrong, Sally insists, it will go wrong with her. She's negative about everything and can't see the bright side of anything. In temperament she's akin to Chicken Little, believing that the world will end and it will probably be today.

Sally can get stuck in a repetitive loop of reciting the woes from her past: her father walked out, she never knew her dad, her mom drank too much. Sally expects bad things to come her way—whether it's getting cut off in traffic or having a bad haircut—and she has very little ability to recognize the blessings in her life.

What one woman might view as a challenge or opportunity, Sally will view as disheartening and discouraging. This may be connected to Sally's experience in the past or it may have to do with her internal emotional wiring. Whatever the source, Sally tends to see the negative in most situations.

That this is how Sally views the world says something about the way she views God. Yes, the world will end one day, but when it does, God's return is going to be good news for those who know Him and trust Him. Our God is all about "Yes!" When Sally views God as a God of "No," she's not seeing the One who is real and true, the God who says yes.

WHEN YOU'RE NOT A SUPERHERO

Are you wondering what man would find Sally attractive enough to marry? I'll tell you who: a superhero. (If you count yourself in this number, it's really not as fantastic as it sounds at first.) This is the guy who wants to "fix" a woman. I've got news for you, though: rarely does this approach to a future mate end well. Women aren't for fixing. Broken cabinet doors are for fixing. Flat tires are for fixing. If there's a woman you want to swoop in and rescue, take her off your list of potential mates.

While I recognize the value in the impulse to fix a person, the reality is often much more complicated. I've seen plenty of guys with a savior complex—who see themselves as knights rescuing a damsel in distress—who are drawn to women who need to be fixed. But most of them find out quickly that they—that you!—do not have the power to fix anyone.

Whatever Sally's issues are, the one person who can effectively address them is Sally.

If you imagine the energy you will bring to a marriage relationship, and the energy Sally will contribute, know that you'll need to bring more than your fair share to keep the ship afloat. And although men considering marriage aren't always thinking ahead to children—which, I'm convinced, is God's design—I encourage you to do just that. Without ever meaning to, with her negative emotional presence Sad Sally will communicate to your future children that they do not bring her joy. They will simply see themselves as another negative in Sally's life.

Because she views the world through this negative filter, guess who else she'll view that way? You! No matter what you do, you'll just be another person who will let Sally down.

Here's what I'd love you to hear: there is One whom Sally must encounter if she is to be transformed, and it's not you. Only God, by the power of His Holy Spirit, can heal and transform and redeem. Psalm 34:18–19 promises:

> The LORD is near to those who have a broken heart,
> And saves such as have a contrite spirit.
> Many are the afflictions of the righteous,
> But the LORD delivers him out of them all.

Be clear: The task of delivering Sally from her sadness and negativity does not have your name on it. Praying that she will experience the radical and transforming grace of God *does*.

EMBRACING LIFE

Sally is a woman without joy. And because she is so obsessed with the pains of her past, she doesn't engage fully with the present. You might think of her as a helium balloon: you constantly have to pump her up, only to find that she is completely deflated the next morning.

The kind of woman who makes the best lifetime partner, Solomon asserted, is a woman who approaches life with energy rather than sadness and negativity. He wrote, "She girds herself with strength, / And strengthens her arms" (Proverbs 31:17). This is the woman who engages her work and the world with gusto and strength.

Elsewhere in Proverbs, Solomon maintained, "A merry heart makes a cheerful countenance, / But by sorrow of the heart the spirit is broken" (15:13). It's not just that Sally wears a frown. The sorrow of her heart has "crushed" her spirit. And sadly, her spirit—which was intended to nurture a husband and children—doesn't do what it was created to do. If you were to picture a bright-red Mylar balloon as a picture of Sally's heart, her sadness has crushed the air out of it, leaving it limp and lifeless on the floor.

The woman who is not crushed by sadness is the one who approaches her work—and who approaches life—vigorously.

HEAD HELD HIGH WHEN TIMES WERE TOUGH

The countertype to Sad Sally isn't Happy Helen. It's not a manically jolly woman with a false smile plastered across her face. The godly woman Solomon said "girds herself with strength" and "strengthens her arms" isn't one who's never faced a bad day. Rather, she's one who faces what comes—the good and the bad—with a spirit that trusts in God no matter her circumstances.

During the twelfth century before Christ, Deborah served as a judge of Israel. Don't imagine her wearing a big black robe and pounding a gavel, though. Ancient judges were a bit different from what you'd imagine today. They would settle disputes and troubleshoot problems between people, and in times of war they'd gather tribes to respond to threats.

Rather than sitting at a judge's bench peering over her reading glasses at an aggressive prosecuting attorney or nervous defendant, Deborah actually sat under a tree in the hill country of Ephraim to serve those who came to her for judgment (Judges 4:4–5). (So I suppose this particular palm tree actually did serve in much the same way as a modern judge's bench.)

The situation in Ephraim at the time was precarious. There was looting of farms and villages, and it had even become unsafe to travel on the highways. When they were threatened by the army of King Jabin, who led the Canaanites, the people turned to Deborah.

Had Deborah responded the way Sad Sally might, she could have said, "The Canaanites have military technology that's superior to ours." Which was true. She might have whined, "But they have a massive, trained professional army." Which was true. She might have moaned, "But they have so many more weapons and chariots than we do." Which was true. She might have groaned, "There's no way we can win. We're doomed." Which certainly appeared to be true.

But Deborah approached life and work with vigor and strong arms. She didn't dwell on the negative, but embraced the possibility of success. She was the kind of charismatic leader, with a fierce faith in God's ability to conquer, who inspired those around her to face challenges with courage and eventually succeed.

Gentlemen, as you consider the woman you will marry, notice if she approaches life with the despondency of a Sad Sally or with the courage and enthusiasm of a Dynamic Deborah.

A VIGOROUS EMBRACE OF LIFE

Kelly is a remarkable young mom who lives around the corner from me. Though I don't know her well, we've spent some time together in social situations. I know that Kelly battled leukemia as a teenager. She married her childhood sweetheart and gave birth to three daughters. When her youngest was two, about three years ago, Kelly was diagnosed with a Stage IV tumor on her liver. She's already outlived the prognosis her doctors had offered her three years ago, and although she had to quit her job as a manager of a local boutique, she continues to care for her daughters at home.

If anyone has just cause to be a Sad Sally, it would be

Kelly. But in the interactions I've had with her over the last few months, and also the encounters our mutual neighbors have shared, Kelly's resilience has been amazing. Her general attitude is, *In life or in death, I trust in God.* She trusts God for the big things, like the span of her life and the futures of her daughters and her husband, but Kelly also trusts God for the smaller daily things: getting a ride home from chemo, knowing someone will prepare dinner for her family, fighting nausea.

Some people who don't know the depth of Kelly's faith might naturally assume she's not in touch with the terrible reality of her situation. Trust me, she is. But despite any earthly circumstance, Kelly has chosen to set her eyes on the One who does not fail.

Gentlemen, I pray the woman you're considering marrying won't have to endure what Kelly has and will. But what you can do right now is notice how a woman interprets the story of her life. No matter what her past, does she understand herself as a victim of circumstance or as a beloved child of God, held in His care?

A TRIUMVIRATE OF WOMEN WHO'VE EMBRACED LIFE

The wife unlike Sad Sally isn't one who's cheerful because she's never faced any obstacles. No, Sally's opposite has endured life's losses, but she hasn't let them define her. I know three women, whose stories overlap a bit, who embody this kind of triumphant spirit. Sharon Daugherty, Lynn Braco, and Constance McLean were all married to high-profile men who were pastoring thriving congregations. Tragically, all three men died in the midst of their ministries. Any of their wives might easily have walked away to nurse their wounds in private. No one would have faulted them for that. Yet all three of these women continued to minister within the congregations their husbands had served and led those churches to thrive even more fully than they had before. Men, look for a woman who has resilience in the face of obstacles.

STOP, PAUSE, OR GO?

You might have a hankering to fix Sally, but if you marry her, you can bet she'll soon be as dissatisfied with you as she is with the rest of the world around her. Stay alert to these telltale signs.

RED FLAG

- She's always complaining about something.
- She thinks everyone else has it better than she does.
- She sees the dark side of most situations.

YELLOW FLAG

- She repeats stories of woe from her past.
- Her happiness depends on *you*.
- She's a woman without joy.

GREEN FLAG

- She has dealt with her past in a healthy way.
- She's fully and vigorously engaged with the present.
- She trusts God to be the steadfast Rock in her life.

She is not afraid of snow for her household,
For all her household is clothed with scarlet.

—

Proverbs 31:21

13

NAVIGATE AWAY FROM NERVOUS NELLIE

I met Nellie when our boys attended the same high school. We'd sit on the bleachers during soccer games under our sun umbrellas and chat mostly about parenting: who had to stay up until midnight finishing a term paper, who asked the pastor's daughter out on a date, who lost his game jersey.

One autumn afternoon during which we clearly did *not* need the umbrellas for sun protection, the dark sky had turned particularly ominous. It was the league quarterfinals, and there were less than two minutes left in the game.

"Now, what's the rule, Mary?" Nellie pressed. "They have to call off the game, right?"

"Well," I guessed, "I don't think they will for dark skies. And I don't think they do for rain. But if the refs see lightning, that's when they call it. I think they'll be able to finish it up, though."

I thought that would be a comfort to my friend, who was prone to worry, but one glance at Nellie's anxious face told me she was not pleased about this at all.

"Well, if it doesn't clear up, I'm taking Carl home," she vowed.

Yikes. I knew how my teenage son would react to that, and I'll just say it wouldn't be pretty.

I reached into my cooler for a bottle of water and offered one to Nellie.

"No, thanks," she declined. "I only drink water that has been triple filtered. But you enjoy it."

Well, it was now about to be a lot less enjoyable than before Nellie had weighed in.

Nellie started digging through the deep recesses of her handbag and resurfaced with a quart of hand sanitizer.

"Here." She thrust it in my direction. "You need this."

Did I? I wasn't eating finger-licking buttery popcorn. I was drinking from a bottle. Though I wasn't certain I needed to scrub with antibacterial gel before drinking a beverage from a container, I politely accepted.

"And make sure you use it to clean around the top," she instructed firmly, dipping back into her purse. "Here's a wipe. Get it really clean. I read those things are just covered with rat droppings."

By this point she'd actually freaked me out enough to wipe the top of the bottle. More than ready to change the subject, I asked if her family had plans for the winter break.

"Well," she began, "we were planning to go to the Grand Canyon. With Carl going off to school next year, it might be the last trip we'll be able to take as a family. But I read that the economy is going to completely implode in two years and the country will fall into ruin. Did you read that?"

"I didn't," I explained. Though if I had, I think I'd be even more inclined to go to the Grand Canyon.

"So I just don't think it would be wise," Nellie continued, "to do something so extravagant when the future is clearly so precarious."

Again, in the event of an unprecedented national or global meltdown, I couldn't think of anything *better* to do than share time together as a family.

"Ooh!" Nellie suddenly gasped as she tracked the action on the field. "Did you see what just happened to my baby?"

I had seen that, with moments left in the game, he had headed the ball down the field to get his team in position to get a goal.

"Yeah, that was great," I raved.

"Not with his *head*, it's not," she corrected me. "I just read this morning that one out of every six million athletes who head the ball will die from concussion-related injuries."

That actually seemed like a comforting statistic to me, but Nellie was clearly troubled. "I read that they're actually developing a helmet now . . ."

Poor Carl. That was all I could think. *Poor Carl.* With any luck, he wouldn't be recruited to play college soccer.

The game was tied, and the play on the field was intense. Only seconds remained. From about twenty yards away from the goal, Carl passed the ball to a teammate and ran straight into position near the goal. The teammate passed it right back, and Carl booted it into the top left corner of the goal, just out of the goalkeeper's reach. As soon as the ball hit the net, the final buzzer sounded.

I glanced at Nellie, and for a moment she actually looked pleased and relaxed.

The crowd jumped up and went wild. Hollering, every player on Carl's team swarmed him and lifted him up on their shoulders as they marched him back to the bench. The players who hadn't been on the field had lifted up a huge watercooler, and when Carl dropped back to earth, they poured it over his head.

When I turned to look at Nellie, she appeared horrified. I knew that if she could have reached Carl in time, she would have made a dash and found a way to prevent the excessive celebration. A face I expected to be delighted was crestfallen and flushed with worry.

During what looked to be the happiest moment of Carl's young life, Nellie, who appeared to be in shock, said only one word.

"Pneumonia."

RACKED WITH ANXIETY

If Sad Sally moves through life with a negative filter, then Nervous Nellie sees the world with an "anxious filter." Truly, she's fearful of everything. She's afraid to drive, afraid to fly, and afraid to try anything new.

She's also obsessed with illness. For Nervous Nellie, there's an injury, disease, or freak infection around every corner. She behaves as if sickness is something to expect and seems completely oblivious to the possibility of living a healthy life.

And just as Sad Sally would be distinguished from someone fighting clinical depression, Nervous Nellie isn't someone with chronic, diagnosable obsessive-compulsive disorder (OCD). Some people caught in an OCD pattern—fixing on one thing incessantly, whether it's repeatedly washing their hands or not being able to leave a room without touching a specific item—truly suffer in the grip of this disease. While there was little help for this type of obsessive behavior years ago, today there is hope for these sufferers.

But I'm not talking about someone with OCD. I'm describing the person gripped with anxiety who seeks no help. This woman would rather continue in the comfort of the anxiety she's grown accustomed to than take the courageous leap to change.

IS SHE THE YIN TO YOUR YANG?

Guys, although you might think that the man who'd be attracted to Nervous Nellie would be as fearful as she is, this isn't necessarily the case. Rather, the kind of guy who is attracted to Nellie is more often a risk taker. If not consciously, something in him recognizes that Nellie balances him out. He senses that she's more structured, more stable. If a guy is a free spirit who aims for the stars, he may choose someone like Nellie who can keep him grounded.

And yet that initial impulse for stability also has the risk of evolving into the very thing that will drive a wedge between him and Nellie. What felt like balance suddenly feels controlling. What seemed like structure becomes suffocating. What was once useful grounding now feels stifling.

Imagine that you're ready to take the leap on a new business venture you've been dreaming of for years. You've created a business plan and have developed a strategy you believe will lead to success. But Nellie is going to balk. She's so averse to financial risk that she'd rather bury your savings in the ground than support the dream you've been given. Jesus actually told a story about someone like that in Matthew 25:14–30. Check it out.

Men, living in fear is not really living. It's the opposite of trusting God for a life that really is alive. It's not what God intended for us when He made us.

Though I realize you probably have other things on your mind right now, I encourage you to, for a moment, think about your eventual children. Do you want them to be raised by a helicopter mom?

NO FEAR WHEN IT SNOWS

When you imagine the terrain of the land that you read about in the Bible, you may be picturing sun and sand. (Jesus wore sandals, right?) However, in about one out of every three years, those who live in Jerusalem actually see snow! There's typically not a lot, but it is cold enough for the powdery white manna from heaven. And in about one out of seven years there will be a snowstorm. So the ancient Near Eastern woman needed to ensure that her family had more to protect them than flip-flops.

Solomon announced of the Good Wife, "She is not afraid of snow for her household, / For all her household is clothed with scarlet" (Proverbs 31:21). Scarlet? Really? Did she buy her kids' ski jackets from Lydia, the savvy entrepreneur with mad tie-dye skills? Is that even important? Well, just as lighter garments are known to repel light and heat, the dark-crimson color was assumed to absorb and retain heat. Solomon was communicating that this woman cared for her family in adverse circumstances.

When the Hebrew texts were translated into Greek, in what was known as the Septuagint, the translation clearly implied that her husband didn't have to be anxious about domestic matters because he knew she had it she had it under control. In case you didn't catch that, Solomon was saying, "Do not marry Nervous Nellie."

I want you to notice the contrast between the two women. Nellie is anxious about all sorts of danger that may or may not happen. When the family of the Good Wife is actually at risk, her husband experiences comfort because his bride—not paralyzed by fear—has taken the steps to protect her family from adversity.

What a striking contrast! In my mind's eye I can see Nellie fretting when she sees snow clouds in the sky. I can hear her bleeding her anxieties onto those around her. Her counterpart, the Good Wife, however, has no fear. She's gotten business done and her family is protected. And when she lives fearlessly, she creates an environment for her husband to do the same.

A FEARLESS MAMA

I want you to use your imagination to think of a woman who would be the polar opposite of the constantly fretting

Nervous Nellie.

- If Nellie is crippled by fear, this woman is not bound by it.
- If Nellie worries over everything, this woman faces even legitimately fearful circumstances with courage.
- If Nellie is terrified as she anticipates injury or illness for her children around every corner, this woman allows her children to face risks with confidence that they are held in God's care.

In the words of Solomon, this woman "is not afraid . . . for her household" (Proverbs 31:21). Pretty different, aren't they?

The woman I've just described is named Jochebed. Jochebed lived in Egypt when the Hebrew people were under oppression there. Yet despite their enslavement, the Hebrew people began to increase in number. Fearful, Pharaoh decreed that all baby boys born to Hebrew women be thrown into the Nile. Could there be a more cowardly decree?

I can't imagine being a Hebrew mother or father during those horrific days. There must have been wailing and weeping in every extended family. When Jochebed knew she was expecting, she must have been torn. In a culture where sons were prized, she surely must have been praying for a daughter. When her child was born—a son—she named him Moses.

I can't imagine how desperate she must have felt about the life of her precious newborn. If anyone had reason to be moved by fear, like Nervous Nellie, it was Jochebed. And yet Jochebed neither allowed her son to be drowned in the Nile nor was crippled by fear. Rather, for three months she nursed Moses and cared for him in secret. During that time, she crafted a courageous plan for the young son she loved.

She also sculpted the most important basket she would ever make. (Many might claim it was the most important container *anyone* would ever make.) Weaving together bulrushes, Jochebed used slime and pitch to make the vessel watertight. No doubt nursing him first, then giving him clean, dry undergarments, Jochebed carefully wrapped her son, lowered him into the basket, and set it adrift in the father of African rivers, regarded as the longest in the world.

Moses, however, did not travel all four-thousand-plus miles. In an absurd twist, he was discovered by the daughter of the Pharaoh who'd ordered his execution. Moved with compassion, she plucked Moses out of the Nile to raise him in Grandpa's own home.

When Pharaoh's daughter pulled Moses from the river, a curious little Hebrew girl sidled up alongside her to peek at the boy. Hidden by tall grasses, his sister, Miriam, had run alongside the floating boy to track his journey. In an age without baby formula, the only way for babies to be nourished was by a mother who was lactating. Miriam offered to find just such a Hebrew woman who could nurse this child.

It's possible Moses never even missed a meal!

Do you recognize the courageous fortitude of Jochebed? Though she must have been terrified for her son, she executed a plan for his welfare as if "she [was] not afraid . . . for her household." Gentlemen, this woman—not Nervous Nellie—is the one to choose as a life partner.

WHAT IT LOOKS LIKE TO LIVE FEARLESSLY

When my boys were younger, Stephanie and I traveled a similar "flight pattern" between home, school, church, and sports. So although we weren't close friends, we'd often chat together as we waited for practice to end or youth group to begin. And although I don't consider myself a Nervous Nellie, I'd say that Stephanie was one of the least nervous women and moms I'd ever met. She was just very grounded.

The first time I noticed it was when her son tripped on the way out of school and came to her with a bloody knee. With concern, she said, "Ouch! You okay, bud?" When it was clear he wasn't upset by the incident, she simply sent him back inside the school to rinse it off and stop the blood with a paper towel, coolly adding, "We'll disinfect and put gauze on it when we get home."

I knew how a Nervous Nellie would have behaved. Her anxiety would have gone through the roof and might even have involved an ambulance.

A few years later, when the boys were in middle school, I saw something similar. One afternoon Stephanie confided in me that in one quarter at school, her son had gone from being a student who got As and Bs to one who got Cs, Ds, and Fs.

I won't lie: I had a moment of feeling like Nervous Nellie when I heard this. But unflappable Stephanie didn't seem rattled by her son's poor performance. I knew she took it seriously and would discover what might be going on with her son, but the news didn't undo her the way that it might have rattled another parent. Stephanie was like a steady ship that couldn't be tossed or thrown off course by life's storms.

Gentlemen, look for a wife who's solidly anchored.

UNFLAPPABLE LORI

One of the most solid women I know, who's as far from Nervous Nellie as you could get, is Lori Bakker, who's married to Jim Bakker. Since her college years, Lori has had serious health issues. As a woman married to a doctor, I'm used to most folks spilling the beans about their medical conditions when they're with Dr. Don. Yet Lori never mentioned hers. Actually, Don and I had to pry it out of Lori that she *had* been suffering for years. She's experienced horrible side effects from previous treatments without complaint.

Anyone who has seen Lori sitting beside Jim on television would have no idea she was hurting. In fact, rather than worrying about herself, Lori would take Jim to the doctor and say, "Doc, I need you to check him over." By God's grace, Don was able to help Lori, and today she's cured of what ailed her. And she continues to be a shining example of the type of woman who doesn't allow anxiety to run her life.

STOP, PAUSE, OR GO?

As with all of the types I'm advising you to avoid, Nellie's nervous habit—which might thrust her into your embrace during scary horror movies—might be endearing right now. But proceed with caution.

RED FLAG

- She sees disaster around every corner.
- She worries about things she cannot control.
- She overreacts to minor situations.

YELLOW FLAG

- She's afraid to try new things.
- She's overly anxious about finances.
- Her fear interferes with her relationships.

GREEN FLAG

- She's solidly grounded in her identity as a beloved child of God.
- She doesn't overreact to minor situations.
- She takes the occasional risk.

A FINAL WORD

So, gentlemen, what do you think? How are you feeling? I suspect there are a few possibilities. If your critical antennae have been piqued, it's possible you're now inspecting your girlfriend's behavior with a crime-scene microscope. Or if you're not dating, it's possible you feel a bit more nervous, concerned there could be a Nellie or a Brenda around every corner. Neither are my intentions. My genuine hope is that, with more tools in your toolbox, you will simply be able to engage with women, eyes wide open, with the sharp wisdom of a serpent and the gentleness of a dove.

First, be wise. I'd encourage you to invite a few folks you trust into an ongoing conversation about the kind of woman you want to marry. As you continue to reflect on the character of the Good Wife, describe for these advisers the type of woman you'd like to marry and communicate to them the types that you're hoping to avoid. Then, if you have the courage—and I hope you do—give your best friend, your

191

brother or sister, and your roommate permission to speak openly and honestly about any woman that you date. That permission requires vulnerability and trust from both of you, but I promise you: it's worth it. The people who love us can be invaluable in giving us a glimpse at our blind spots.

Second, be gentle. Though you may be on the prowl for "the perfect woman," remember that every one of us comes with sin and brokenness that the Lord is in the process of redeeming. Because you know what those areas are in your own life, and how wily some of our sins and wounds can be, extend the same generosity and compassion to each woman you meet that you'd expect her to extend to you.

I'm advising you to avoid the woman who has allowed sin to take up residence in her life in such a way that it *defines* who she is. If you're looking for a perfect woman, you can anticipate many lonely years ahead. But as you're willing to ask God to give you His vision for the woman you are to marry, you'll recognize the perfectly imperfect woman that God has for you.

Beloved brothers and sons, wise and gentle, I pray that God will lead you to the woman with whom you will be able to share a life that will glorify Him forever.

ABOUT THE AUTHOR

Mary Colbert is the wife of Dr. Don Colbert. One of eight children raised in a military home, she has a unique insight into different kinds of personalities that prepared her well for ministry. Now with two sons, six grandsons, and one grand-daughter, Mary has thought deeply about the types of women she wants her boys to wed and the kind of wife she wants her granddaughter to be.

Mary attended Oral Roberts University, where she met her husband of thirty-five years. She graduated from Rhema Bible School and is an ordained minister. She coauthored the New York Times bestseller *Seven Pillars of Health* with her husband and serves as vice president of Divine Health Nutritional Company. The Colberts live in Orlando, Florida.

WORTHY

If you enjoyed this book, will you consider sharing the message with others?

- Mention the book in a Facebook post, Twitter update, Pinterest pin, blog post, or upload a picture through Instagram.
- Recommend this book to those in your small group, book club, workplace, and classes.
- Head over to Facebook.com/worthypublishing, "LIKE" the page, and post a comment as to what you enjoyed the most.
- Tweet "I recommend reading #13WomenYouShould NeverMarry by @marydoncolbert // @worthypub"
- Pick up a copy for someone you know who would be challenged and encouraged by this message.
- Write a book review online.

You can subscribe to Worthy Publishing's
newsletter at worthypublishing.com.